KIRI TE KANAWA
A Biography

KIRI TE KANAWA

A Biography

DAVID FINGLETON

Foreword by James Levine

Music Director and Principal Conductor
of The Metropolitan Opera

ATHENEUM

New York

1983

Library of Congress Cataloging in Publication Data
Fingleton, David.
    Kiri Te Kanawa.
    Includes index.
    1. Te Kanawa, Kiri. 2. Singers—Biography.
I. Title.
ML420.T26F5   1983   782.1'092'2   [B]   82-73013
ISBN 0-689-11345-5

Manufactured by Fairfield Graphics, Fairfield, Pennsylvania
First American Edition

CONTENTS

ILLUSTRATIONS

between pages

With Boris Christoff in *Boris Godunov* (*Donald Southern*)
In *The Marriage of Figaro* (*Zoe Dominic*)
Jean Mallandaine, role coach (*Philip Ingram*)
At New Zealand House, London, with the late Lord Ballantrae
A Face for the Seventies (*Snowdon*)
With Jon Vickers in *Otello*, New York (*Roy Jones*)
With Placido Domingo in *Carmen* (*Reg Wilson*)
After the gala premiere of *Carmen* at Covent Garden (*Donald Southern*)
In *Otello* at Covent Garden with Carlo Cossutta (*Reg Wilson*)
Rehearsing *Faust* with John Copley and Stuart Burrows (*Anthony Crickmay*)
As Marguerite in *Faust* (*Donald Southern*)
A reception at the Paris Opéra (*Gamma, Paris*)
With Luciano Pavarotti and Thomas Allen in *La Bohème* (*Reg Wilson*)
As Tatiana in *Eugene Onegin* (*Donald Southern*)
With Desmond, Basil Horsfield and Sam Niefeld (*Bill Double*)

Kiri in 1976 (*Bill Double*)   128-129
In *Così fan tutte* at the Paris Opéra (*Michel Szabo, Boissy-Saint-Leger*)
Cobber the cat
Relaxing at home (*John Downing, Daily Express*)
With Desmond and daughter Toni, aged two (*Bill Double*)
A difficult audience (*John Downing, Daily Express*)
With Mirella Freni during the filming of *The Marriage of Figaro* (*Karl Bayer, Garmisch*)
In *Arabella* at Covent Garden (*Clive Barda*)
Rehearsing *Die Fledermaus* with Hermann Prey (*Christina Burton*)
With conductor Zubin Mehta (*Christina Burton*)
As Violetta in *La Traviata* at the Sydney Opera House (*Branco Gaica, Sydney*)
With director Joseph Losey during filming of *Don Giovanni* (*Pierluigi/Rex*)

As Donna Elvira in the film *Don Giovanni* (*Gaumont Films*)

Rehearsing a concert with conductor Claudio Abbado (*Photo Ellinger, Salzburg*)

As a surprise 'guest' in *Die Fledermaus* at Covent Garden (*Paul Smith*)

As Pamina in *The Magic Flute* with Stuart Burrows (*Clive Barda*)

Playing golf with Placido Domingo, Bernard Levin and Sir John Tooley (*Clive Barda*)

On the golf course (*Clive Barda*)

With Dame Joan Sutherland and Angela Lansbury (*Clive Barda*)

With Sir Georg Solti at a recording of *The Marriage of Figaro* (*Clive Barda*)

With Frederica von Stade at the recording session (*Clive Barda*)

Rehearsing *Don Giovanni* with Peter Wood, Sir Colin Davis and Ruggero Raimondi (*Clive Barda*)

As Donna Elvira in the Covent Garden production of *Don Giovanni* (*Clive Barda*)

Singing 'Let the Bright Seraphim' in St Paul's cathedral (*Adam Woolfitt, Daily Telegraph*)

With Desmond, Toni and Thomas on *This Is Your Life* (*Thames Television*)

As Tosca at the Paris Opéra (*Daniel Cande, Boulogne*)

FOREWORD

It is exceedingly rare to find in one person an exceptional voice, a beautiful woman, a striking stage personality and a real human being —passionate, sensitive, amusing and continually enigmatic. But all these qualities combine to make Kiri what she is today. She is not only an artist in world demand, but also a person whose company is warm, stimulating and ultimately rewarding because she values her private life at least as much as her career. I first worked with her in 1974 at the Metropolitan Opera in Verdi's *Otello*. She made her debut on three hours' notice in a live radio broadcast, substituting for an indisposed colleague. Her beauty, presence and the singular quality of her voice astonished and excited the audience immediately, and it was one of those extraordinary moments in the opera house when one can sense the audience's discovery of a new "star." Since then we have collaborated on *Così fan tutte* and *Der Rosenkavalier*, and her work and her personality continue to fascinate me as she continues to develop and grow. Considering how extraordinary are her gifts and how much pleasure she has given to so many while still so young, one can only be keenly excited by the almost infinite possibilities that her future development will afford.

JAMES LEVINE
Music Director and Principal Conductor of
The Metropolitan Opera
December 1, 1982

PREFACE

THERE WAS NOTHING UNUSUAL in itself about a telephone call to New Zealand soprano Kiri Te Kanawa in Paris from her agent, Basil Horsfield, in London. He and his partner, John Davern, have managed Kiri's career since the end of her student days in London in the late 1960s and, wherever in the world she may be, they keep in constant touch to discuss present and future engagements, rehearsal and recording schedules, and the inevitable last-minute changes of plan in a crowded diary which has to be planned up to five years ahead. In April 1981 Kiri was in Paris to sing a series of performances in the title role of Richard Strauss's *Arabella*, being heard for the first time at the Paris Opéra, and to record Berlioz's song-cycle *Les Nuits d'Été* with Daniel Barenboim and l'Orchestre de Paris. Both opera performances and recording sessions had gone splendidly and she was in ebullient form. She laughs now when she remembers that telephone conversation.

'Kiri,' said Horsfield, 'first I've got some good news – Charles has asked you to sing at his wedding.'

'Charles who? I don't think I know any Charleses.'

'Yes you do – Prince Charles,' was Horsfield's reply, and Kiri could only gasp 'Oh God!'

Three months later the congregation of St Paul's Cathedral, plus some 600 million television viewers world-wide – 'approximately 250,000 Covent Garden audiences at the same time', NBC's interviewer Tom Brokaw had pointed out to her the week before – heard and saw Kiri Te Kanawa sing 'Let the bright seraphim' from Handel's oratorio *Samson* while the Prince and Princess of Wales signed the wedding register.

Opinions differed afterwards about her multi-coloured, primarily yellow, high-necked dress with its ruched collar, and the funny little peacock-blue silk hat that perched on top of her wavy, dark-blonde hair: there were those who found the outfit suitably operatic, and others who were less enthusiastic. Fellow antipodean Clive James, writing in the following Sunday's *Observer*, had the nerve to describe it as 'what may have been the last surviving example of the Maori national dress'.

But there were no disagreements about the sheer quality of her voice. 'Heaven was brushed by Maori soprano Kiri Te Kanawa's dome-splitting top A,' wrote Jean Rook in the *Daily Express*; 'Thoughtfully, HRH had left Kiri Te Kanawa behind to thrill us,' commented the *Guardian*; 'The only sounds as brilliant as the Trumpet Voluntary were the bell-like notes of New Zealand's Kiri Te Kanawa,' was the *Daily Mail*'s view; and Philip Howard, writing in *The Times*, observed 'That bright seraph, Kiri Te Kanawa, filled the great dome with celestial concerts in harmony with the orchestra and massed choirs.' Only 'Denis Thatcher' writing to 'Dear Bill' in *Private Eye* complained that 'This dusky songstress from Down Under in a multi-coloured tablecloth and air hostess's hat warbles on for bloody hours' – and that in itself was fame of a kind.

She deserved the tributes: it was a magnificent, joyful performance, the voice clear as a bell, effortlessly filling the cathedral, and giving no hint at all of the exhaustion she actually felt after an unprecedented seven performances as Donna Elvira in *Don Giovanni* plus four as Fiordiligi in *Così fan Tutte* in the previous three weeks, during the Royal Opera's Mozart Festival.

The following day Kiri received a telegram from Buckingham Palace. It read: OUR WARMEST THANKS FOR YOUR SUPERB SINGING AT TODAY'S CEREMONY. YOUR PERFORMANCE DID SO MUCH TO MAKE IT

SUCH A HAPPY AND MEMORABLE OCCASION. CHARLES AND DIANA. Not bad for the girl from Gisborne on the North Island of New Zealand, who had come to London to train at the London Opera Centre in 1966 and in just fifteen years had become one of the leading, most sought-after sopranos in the world.

I

Early Days in Gisborne

TOM AND NELL TE KANAWA had been married and living in Gisborne for some years before their daughter, Kiri, arrived. Nell's family, the Leeces, had come to New Zealand from the Isle of Man at the end of the nineteenth century. Her great-uncle had been the famous English composer Sir Arthur Sullivan: musical awareness was thus already there, and most members of the New Zealand Leece family had played one instrument or another in North Country brass bands. Nell's sister had apparently played the cornet beautifully, and she herself was a competent pianist.

Nell had been married twice before in New Zealand to men of white descent. By her first marriage she had two children, a son and a daughter, Nola, who is today in her sixties and looks after her step-father when he is at home in New Zealand. The second had been extremely short-lived and had left her in disgrace, both with her family and with the Roman Catholic Church, of which she was a member: there had even been talk of excommunication. But when she married the Maori Tom Te Kanawa in 1938 there were no complaints, for the Te Kanawa tribe was a princely one whose past was steeped in Maori history and legend. They came from the King Country, near Mount Egmont in the North Island, and their village was Te Kuiti where the famous tourist attraction of Waitomo Caves had been discovered, it was said, by a Te Kanawa ancestor chasing a lost pig. He found the errant beast in a cave, and thus discovered Waitomo. As a teenager Kiri visited the caves with a boyfriend and, when she sang a Maori song in one vaulted, cathedral-like cave discovered it had perfect acoustics. Another piece of Te Kanawa folk-lore concerns the chief who had a tender affair with a fairy on Mount Pukemoremore. The fairy used to spend her nights with him, then fly off before the first light of dawn. Te Kanawa decided he might be able to hang on to her for ever if he blocked out all the light in his hut. It nearly worked, but when the sun was fully up a chink of light got through and the beautiful fairy awoke. She flew sadly away through the roof, pausing only for a farewell love song – naturally she had an exquisite voice – and never returned. It could almost have made the libretto for an opera.

Tom and Nell Te Kanawa lived a rather less romantic life in Gisborne on the East coast of the North Island overlooking Poverty Bay, so-called because the redoubtable Captain Cook had not found the natives friendly when he arrived there. Tom had worked on building the road to Gisborne through the gorge from Whakatane and afterwards had set up a truck-contracting business. In their large rambling house Nell let out rooms to students, for she always liked to have young people around her. They were both extremely fond of children and dearly wished for a son of their own. But Nell was now in her forties: it was too late for her to have any more children. So the Te Kanawas placed their name on an adoption list and also advertized in the local paper – for a boy. In April 1944 a social worker came to the house with a five-week-old baby girl, but the Te Kanawas turned the offer down. The social worker returned with the baby, however, and Tom remembers saying to his wife, 'Look at that poor little girl – she's got no home. Poor kid, no-one's adopted her yet.' Nell, knowing that it was actually Tom who was so keen to have a son, said, 'Well, it's up to you.' So the baby girl was taken in and named after Tom's father, Kiri, the Maori word for Bell.

Kiri had been born on 6 March 1944 to parents who were, appropriately, of the same racial mix as the Te Kanawas: her mother was of European origin and her father a Maori. Though her mother remained faithful to him throughout her life, they never married and were extremely poor. Her mother had been a non-conformist minister's daughter, hence the disgrace and ostracism. The couple also had a son who, it is said, used to listen to his younger sister singing on the radio; but to Kiri's knowledge they have never met. It was also said that Kiri's father had a glorious silver tenor voice but, as Kiri remarks now, 'When you're an adopted opera singer your father's just got to have a silver tenor voice!' He died of tuberculosis at the age of thirty-five. Kiri never met him nor her mother, who died just a few years ago in Australia. She has never really tried to find any of her original family though she thinks she may have met some of them unwittingly in New Zealand. 'Nobody's ever said a word. When a Maori child is given away you're not meant to say anything or ever try to retrieve it. That's rather beautiful, really.'

Kiri's earliest memories of life with her new parents in Gisborne are of an enormous house perpetually full of people. Nell, being a gregarious woman, liked nothing better than to fill the place with parties and sing-songs. In addition to the students there was also old Uncle Dan, who had retired and lived in a top bedroom which he called his 'office'. 'Would you like to come to my office,' he would say to Kiri when her parents were out, and she appreciates now that he was effectively her Nannie. She was only two when her parents told her that she had been adopted, as a secret between her and them. They suggested it would be better if she did not tell her friends when she went to school. 'It turned me into a survivor: I felt I was special and had special responsibilities. I'm quite sure if I hadn't known I was adopted I'd have stayed a nobody and would be in New Zealand breeding children now. But that turned me into a fighter.'

At the age of five Kiri started at the local school but even before that there had been little sing-songs with her mother at the piano, beginning, as she recalls, with 'Daisy, Daisy'. 'Looking back on it now,' she says 'I can see Mummy constantly kept the music going. I'd tend not to feel like it because I was a lazy child, but she'd insist that I sang, and by the time I was eight she could hear that I could sing pretty well.' By then she had even had her first taste of singing in public.

Gisborne had a local radio station, 2XG, on which a much-loved old lady known as Aunt Daisy ran a sort of talent spotting show for young people every summer. As Kiri remembers, 'I can't have been more than six when I first went on it. I remember singing "Daisy, Daisy", of course, and "When I grow too old to dream", which I still love, and even some Victorian ballads. I recall going on the show once with a very bad cold, so I cracked on a note. I was very embarrassed, and somebody else who was there laughed. It was my first sobering experience of anybody being jealous.'

Nell was becoming so impressed by her daughter's vocal potential that she decided the time had come for something to be done. She had heard that at St Mary's College for Girls at Ponsonby in Auckland – a convent school – there was a renowned singing teacher called Sister Mary Leo who had been a singer and instrumentalist herself and had produced operas and concerts before becoming a Sister of Mercy. She ran the music school at St Mary's and her pupils tended to carry off all the singing prizes in New Zealand, and many of those in Australia too. So Mrs Te Kanawa telephoned Sister Mary Leo in Auckland and, being the confident woman she was, announced, 'I have a daughter who sings very well – will you take her on?' The Sister replied that Kiri couldn't start with her until she was eighteen. But Nell was not so easily put off; she decided there and then that if the family moved to Auckland and Sister Mary Leo were confronted by her gifted daughter, she might be persuaded. It was typical of Nell Te Kanawa's character to take the initiative in this way. Up to her departure for England, to study at the London Opera Centre, Kiri would find time and again that her mother managed to surmount apparently insuperable difficulties to organize something that she believed needed to be done to further her daughter's career. She always seemed to know just the right person – journalist, businessman or politician – and could be quite fearless in their pursuit. Together,

[18]

she and Tom ensured that Kiri had an enormously happy childhood and adolescence, giving her a vital sense of security that would stand her in such stead against the pressures of success that lay ahead.

So Nell made two trips to Auckland to look for a house and eventually found one in Mitchell Street, overlooking Blockhouse Bay, a suburb about nine miles from the centre. For the Te Kanawa family the proposed move was quite an upheaval. Their large house in Gisborne had to be sold, and Tom's truck business disposed of (once in Auckland he found work installing petrol tanks for Caltex). Money was a problem too: there would no longer be the income from letting rooms, and there were all the expenses of the move to be met. But Nell was convinced that they would manage somehow, and that it would all be worth it if Kiri could be professionally taught to sing by the best singing teacher in New Zealand. They moved in 1956 when Kiri was twelve, and she recalls a very sad twelfth birthday, made more solemn by the fact that once in Auckland she was confirmed almost immediately in the local Roman Catholic Church. Initially she was sent to a primary school near Avondale, and moved on to St Mary's when she was fourteen.

2

Sister Mary Leo and Johnny Waititi

WHEN KIRI MOVED UP to St Mary's College in 1958 she still had not met Sister Mary Leo – that had been left to mother. Her first experience of the Sister came when she was called out of class to the Music School, a two-storey house in the school's grounds in which Sister Mary Leo had a beautiful, sunny L-shaped room decorated with busts of composers and, on and around the piano, numerous framed photographs of successful pupils.

The small wiry nun, with sharp eyes behind spectacles and an air of quiet authority – who 'seemed enormously old to me even then, and she's still alive and fit, and teaching today, twenty-four years later!' – made an initially daunting impression on Kiri. Sister Mary Leo found her very shy at first, and not yet prepared for the hard work that would be essential for musical achievement. As she puts it, 'She required encouragement and guidance to reach the sense of purpose which any serious singer needs, and gradually she developed this quality. At that time Kiri was more attracted to lighter music, anything pleasant, popular and tuneful, which required less effort to master.' Nell also knew about this lack of application; still determined that her daughter would become a serious singer, she took her to see operatic performances in Auckland, of Mozart's *The Magic Flute* and *Don Giovanni*. Kiri remembers enjoying them well enough but admits they made no great impression on her. She certainly didn't appreciate then that both operas had parts that lay precisely right for her voice, and that one day she would be singing the roles of Pamina and Donna Elvira to international acclaim.

Sister Mary Leo recognized that 'it was mainly her mother's wish and ambition on Kiri's behalf which led her to devote herself chiefly to more serious music; certainly I felt her voice was much too good to be spent on music of an essentially trivial kind.' Kiri agrees she was lazy to begin with, but she came to appreciate, rather than to fear, being called out of ordinary lessons to go to Sister Leo's music room. 'She had first call on any student she wanted; at first I practised little folk songs – opera wasn't mentioned. She had an unorthodox teaching method, and even nowadays I sometimes find myself subconsciously slipping back to her style of breathing. It wasn't wrong for me then, but it is now. Above all, though, like my present teacher Vera Rozsa, she has a marvellous ear, and the greatest gift I received from her was her constant attention.'

Kiri remained at St Mary's for two years, receiving two singing lessons with Sister Mary Leo most weeks, singing in the school choir and taking solos: 'All sorts of things – I particularly remember as an early effort the Nuns' Chorus from *Casanova* by Johann Strauss.' This in fact became one of her first recordings in New Zealand, for Kiwi Records, and very good it sounds still, with the effortlessly soaring sweetness of her voice already there although, as Sister Leo thought, a more mezzo quality was noticeable. (Indeed the full potential of Kiri's upper range was not to be discovered and exploited until after she came to England; when she entered the London Opera Centre, it was as a mezzo soprano.)

Next door to the Te Kanawas at their new home in Mitchell Street lived a large family, the Hansons. The father was a businessman; he and his wife had six sons and later adopted a daughter as well. Amongst the sons was one of almost exactly Kiri's age, Robert, who has remained one of her closest friends. He is now an architect practising in London and still vividly remembers their first meeting.

'We used to see this pretty girl walking up and down the drive every day, going to get the morning paper. We could see she was looking at us, and one morning one of my brothers waved – and she waved back. Knowing Kiri now it doesn't surprise me – it did then!' Up to that point they knew nothing about her at all, except that she had a Maori father and that trucks would come up and down the drive. The families got to know one another. 'We were adopted by Kiri as her de facto family,' says Robert, 'and I got to know hers very well too, especially her mother, who was a wonderful, warm-hearted person. She was outwardly aggressive but if you knew how to handle her, she was soft as butter. Most people called her "boss", but personally I called her "Ma".' Robert Hanson soon realized that for all Tom's quiet interest in and obvious love for his daughter, it was the much more extrovert Nell who took the big decisions in the family, and that it was she who was determined that Kiri was going to become a successful singer.

On the academic front Kiri had been making rather slower progress than at music and was not thought good enough by her teachers to take GCE 'O' levels. That being so, she left St Mary's at the age of sixteen and entered a business college to learn shorthand and typing. When Kiri completed the course there was no question of full-time preparation for a musical career; there was simply insufficient money available at that stage, and in any case, Kiri still lacked motivation; as she herself puts it now, 'Nothing was really established by then – I was still floating.' Her parents had given her a battered Standard 8 for her sixteenth birthday. During college days, getting out and having fun with the Hanson boys and other teenage residents of Blockhouse Bay, swimming, sailing and skiing, were what she enjoyed most. Despite her early departure from St Mary's, though, Nell remained determined that her daughter should continue her lessons with Sister Mary Leo, and it was from this time, says Kiri, that 'despite having half the energy, and being twice as lazy as I am now' her career as a singer began to take shape.

One of Kiri's friends at St Mary's had been Raewyn Blade, later to become much closer to her once they were both in London, and today the New Zealand friend whom she sees most frequently. Raewyn is now an established stage and television singer and actress (as well as 'Miss New Zealand Lamb' in television commercials) and she too studied with Sister Mary Leo. She recalls Kiri's interest in light music in those days, 'before she'd won any competitions or anything. We went into an amateur production of *The Student Prince*. Kiri was covering the lady who sang "Just we two", and I remember thinking then "what an amazing sound".' Shortly after that Kiri and Raewyn both took chorus roles in an Auckland production of *Annie Get Your Gun* at the King's Theatre. 'Annie' – Anne Hart – now married to comedian Ronnie Corbett, had been flown out from England; one of Kiri's jobs was to hand her the guns. It was all good fun, and possibly useful stage experience, but the wage was a meagre £19 per week which wasn't going to take her life or studies very far. In order better to earn her living Kiri next took a job as an operator in Auckland's telephone exchange on the basis that its shift system would leave her enough time to continue singing lessons with Sister Mary. But it wasn't a success. 'The time I got up to do the early shift was 6 a.m. I worked till 1 p.m., which left me exhausted and without much time left for singing. So I tried the night shift, and that was even worse: it meant I had to get up at two in the morning – they were terrible, terrible hours. But I had to figure out a way of continuing singing as well as bringing in money, as I had none of my own.'

So next she went to work in an Auckland music store, selling sheet music. This had been her mother's idea. 'She thought I should get to know a lot about music, the names of composers and so on, which I did.' Unfortunately the elder of the two women who ran the shop turned out to be a very difficult employer, who would keep Kiri standing up all day, which ultimately caused varicose vein problems and led to Kiri needing to have one stripped at the age of nineteen. After about six months she told her mother she could stand no more, and left. She comments now, 'That old woman was really horrible to me then but, of course, like so many other people, after I'd become successful she was fine.'

[23]

The next job was far more congenial, though it was still one that did very little to advance her singing career. Through her father Tom's connections she was taken on as a receptionist at the Auckland office of Caltex Petroleum. This was much more fun, as it gave Kiri the chance to meet everybody coming in and out of the office and her friends could pop in to chat. The salary was small, but enough to keep her in hairdos and dresses. In addition, the job also enabled her to see Sister Mary Leo more regularly, though still at that stage to no great effect. 'In the lunch hour I'd catch a taxi up to St Mary's, have thirty minutes with Sister Mary, and do basically nothing.' While at Caltex she did, however, begin to earn a little money from singing. Raewyn explains, 'The only professional work you could do was cabaret, or "dine and dance" as they called it in New Zealand. The places would be about twenty miles apart, and you would disappear in a little old car and come back at two in the morning, having done three gigs, totally exhausted.' Kiri now embarked on these, as well as singing at the occasional wedding – and on Saturdays, if she fitted in three or four clubs, plus a wedding, she could earn about £25. These clubs were enormously sedate and respectable by current European standards: 'Like a dining and dancing club of a family type, and very dignified. My parents saw the people I was working with and agreed to let me do it, and I'd sing a couple of songs and go home. At that stage I was always the first one on – not top of the bill at the end – and in any case the place closed at twelve.'

For these early engagements Kiri's repertoire was strictly non-operatic. Another friend at that time, who was later to be chief bridesmaid at Kiri's wedding, was Sally Rush, now Sally Sloman. She too was studying with Sister Mary Leo as well as training to be a 'Karitane' children's nurse. Sally remembers, 'Kiri would collect me from the nurses' home in her blue car, and we'd have fun racing round the city on Saturday nights to various engagements at quite select nightclubs and coffee houses. Her favourite songs at that time were "Granada" and "Summertime".' Sally also recalls that at private parties she and Kiri were in some demand for a double act entitled 'Herbie the Surfie'. Kiri herself explains that 'The public at those places were very basic; opera, even Gilbert and Sullivan, didn't go down at all well. They wanted things they knew, and the latest hits. So I sang "The hills are alive with the sound of music" and "Climb every mountain" from *The Sound of Music*, "Maria" from *West Side Story*, and "I could have danced all night" from *My Fair Lady*.'

Much more recently, in 1980 and 1981, Kiri was still scoring hits with two of these songs. In January 1980 at Covent Garden, the last performance of Johann Strauss's operetta *Die Fledermaus* was a charity gala performance in the presence of the Queen Mother. When the production was new, two years earlier, Kiri had been the original Rosalinde; this time she had agreed to appear at Prince Orlofsky's second-act party as part of the cabaret to help the good cause. Young baritone Jonathan Summers, playing Falke and acting as master of ceremonies, announced, 'Now Miss Kiri Te Kanawa will sing "Sempre libera" from *La Traviata*' – the role Kiri was in fact performing at Covent Garden that month. On walked Kiri leading an enormous white goat that she had borrowed from Chessington Zoo. Wearing lederhosen, a Tyrolean hat and her blond wig in two outrageously horizontal pigtails, she advanced to the footlights, peered down at conductor Peter Maag and wailed, 'Oh no maestro, not that again!' Instead she launched into 'Climb every mountain' and, following tumultuous applause, delivered 'The lonely goatherd', complete with yodelling, as an encore. The Queen Mother looked enraptured.

When, that autumn, there was another Covent Garden cabaret, this time before a vast auction to raise funds for the Opera House's new extension, Kiri's early talents were called on again. This time she delivered 'I could have danced all night' waltzing around a model of the Rolls Royce Corniche that was to be the auction's prize lot later in the evening. Once again she brought the house down, and the following spring sang the song again in the presence of the Prince of Wales at the gala opening of the restored Palace Theatre in Manchester. Anybody who was at any of those supremely spontaneous, happy and energetic performances would have realized just what it was that so endeared Kiri to her compatriots in New Zealand in those early days, and might have reflected how easily her career could in fact have taken quite a different direction. Indeed in Auckland in the early 1960s it wasn't long before her cabaret career took off. At the same time came success as a recording artist, and performances in and around Auckland with the extremely popular comedy singing duo of Lou and Simon, who still remember Kiri with the utmost fondness, not only for her talent but also for her great sense of fun. But, successful as Kiri was fast becoming, Nell's view was that things couldn't go on like this indefinitely.

Nell needed a guardian angel for her talented daughter and found one in Johnny Waititi, a founder and one of the governors of the Maori Trust Foundation. The foundation had been set up to provide for the further education of any Maori child who had promise, but Kiri explains, 'It was mainly for the academic, rather than the musical child, and I certainly wasn't academic! But I was still short of money for full-time studying, so many parents applied to the Trust. There were enormous problems: people felt, why should they give the money to someone who was already successful and could run around in a car, and that sort of thing. But fortunately Johnny knew I had talent and that Mummy and Daddy didn't have all that much money. The grant wasn't a lot, at most about £250, but it paid for a year's singing lessons and that meant I could stop doing a job just to earn enough to pay for them.'

But first Kiri's parents wanted to be sure that their faith in their daughter, and indeed Johnny Waititi's, would be justified. Robert Hanson's mother, Betty Hanson, recalls, 'Ma had great faith in Kiri and a definite idea of where she thought Kiri was going, certainly that she was going to develop the gift with which she was born. Her attitude was that it was Kiri's responsibility to do everything she could to develop that gift. Ma did her utmost for Kiri, because she saw that being part-Maori might otherwise be her downfall! Kiri had this happy-go-lucky attitude and Ma was the disciplinarian. Kiri owes a tremendous amount to her. I remember

[26]

going with some American friends to Tom and Nell's house on Lake Taupo when Kiri was only fifteen or sixteen. We'd told them about her voice and, naturally, they wanted to hear Kiri sing. But as it was a sunny day and she was enjoying herself out of doors, Kiri didn't want to oblige. But Ma, the disciplinarian stood firm: "You have a God-given voice which gives people pleasure – it's your duty to show them," she told her daughter, and Kiri duly sang some Maori songs, quite beautifully, without even a piano to accompany her.'

When Kiri's parents put Johnny Waititi's proposal to her, Kiri's reaction was enthusiastic. 'I remember it vividly: they came to collect me one afternoon from Caltex. We sat in the car outside, and mummy and daddy said, "We want to talk to you very seriously, Kiri." I said, "Yes, OK" as seriously as you can as a teenager, and then they said, "You've got just one chance – either you sing or you just keep working at Caltex. It's one or the other, but whatever you do, you've got to do it totally." I said, "OK, I'll take it – let's give it a go." And from then on I haven't stopped.'

Kiri became immensely fond of Johnny Waititi, and remains grateful and devoted to him to this day. Sadly, she was not to know him for long. 'I loved him so much; he was my hero, and looking back on it now, he was the major factor in my beginning life as a professional singer. Because of Johnny, too, I came to feel more Maori myself and was proud of it. But just a couple of years after I got the grant, when I was about to leave for the competitions in Australia on my first international flight, Johnny telephoned and said he wanted to see me. He was in hospital. I told him I was just leaving for the airport but that I'd try to get to him on the way. But I knew I couldn't because I was running so late, and so I missed him. A few days later in Australia I had a letter saying he'd died – of leukaemia. He was only forty. I knew he used to complain of pains in his back and I used to drive him around in the car just so that he wouldn't be in pain, but I'd no idea I was going to lose him so soon. He was so very important in my life.'

3

Competitions and Prizes

FOR KIRI THE ROUTE to a successful musical career lay not only in regular study with Sister Mary Leo – tremendous effort, and sustained sessions of training, coaching and practice – but also, to put this hard work to good use, in entering the various singing competitions which then abounded in New Zealand, and indeed in Australia. The finals of such competitions were generally tied in with radio broadcasts and these, together with subsequent recordings of the winner's efforts, were the way in which talent was 'spotted' and further study abroad might be achieved. Kiri's first major success came in the Auckland Competition of 1960, when she was sixteen – and was chosen as the most promising new voice. A by-product of that particular success had been the loss of her boyfriend, a young man several years older than her but evidently rather less wise. 'I remember he rang up, and I said that I'd got these tickets for the prize-winners' concert and that I'd love him to come and hear me sing, as he never had. He replied that if I went in for the concert he never wanted to see me again. It had never entered my head that anyone was going to try and stop me, so I just said goodbye and slammed down the receiver. I went ahead and did the concert and sang "Road to the Isles" in what sounds now a very young voice, though I suppose that even if I didn't feel it was particularly wonderful, for my age my voice did have more maturity and volume than most.'

By 1963, under Sister Mary Leo's careful and constant super-vision, Kiri's voice was truly beginning to expand and mature beyond its initially more mezzo-soprano range. Sister Leo's view of Kiri at that time is that, 'Once success came her way she was more ready to work hard and improve her attainments. She was co-operative and prepared to accept guidance. As her character and voice developed, she formed her own ideas on performance and interpretation, but she never persisted in thinking they were in-variably right. Through her co-operation and our discussion we would evolve what seemed to be the right style and appropriate attitude for her in any given musical situation. As she grew older, her approach to singing became more mature – and she had already developed a charming stage personality, with warm audience appeal.' If, alongside her work with Sister Mary Leo, Kiri's nightclub and recording engagements were not expanding her repertoire or testing her technique, they did at least add greatly to her confidence before an audience.

The most important and prestigious singing competition in New Zealand at that time was the Mobil Song Quest. The Mobil Petroleum Company had started to sponsor the competition in 1956: it took place every other year in one of New Zealand's major cities. Slightly to her surprise, particularly when she heard the recording broadcast on the radio at home, Kiri passed triumphantly through the semi-final heat in Auckland with 'Come to the Fair' and 'She is Far From the Land', and was thus invited to take part in the final in Hamilton, further south on the North Island.

Once she arrived Mobil took over and gave Kiri her first taste of being treated like a prima donna. The finalists were lodged in the town's principal hotel and she found herself being interviewed by the media, receiving bouquets at the hotel from unknown ad-mirers and being chauffeured to and from Founders' Hall where the final was taking place. The competitors on stage sang, with orchestral accompaniment, to an audience in the hall and were broadcast live. The judges listened, not in the audience, but to the radio broadcast at Radio Centre on the other side of town, and thus reached their

[29]

verdicts on the singers' sound alone. James Robertson, soon to become first Director of the newly established London Opera Centre (under the auspices of the Royal Opera House in London) was in New Zealand working with the New Zealand Opera Company and was the principal judge at Hamilton for the 1963 Song Quest. He still remembers the final clearly, as well he might, for just three years later Kiri came to the Opera Centre as a student, and has since been regarded as that establishment's star pupil.

'I did it by sound and it very quickly came down to two singers: one was Kiri, the other Malvina Major. I gave it to Malvina; it was very close, but she was the more classical singer at that stage. The audience was slightly surprised, but I was sure I was right. Kiri had a superlative natural talent, though, and as soon as I met her I could see that her looks were to be added to the beautiful creamy sound she made.' The audience who had applauded Kiri to the echo in Founders' Hall had, of course, had the advantage of seeing her looks and stage manner there and then, and clearly for them this striking, tall slim girl with dark wavy hair, enormous brown eyes and glowing bronze-coloured skin was already well on her way to stardom.

Although she was disappointed not to have won Kiri gained enormous confidence from her experience as runner-up, and from the ballyhoo that followed the contest: several receptions around town, at which she found herself adored by total strangers who were all convinced she should have won, did much for her morale. The following afternoon she travelled back to Auckland for the final of the John Court aria competition there that evening. Feeling well below par as a result of the excitement and celebrations of the previous night, she sang 'The Tryst' by Sibelius and went straight home to bed, convinced that once again she would at best be only runner-up. At midnight she was woken by a telephone call from her friend Ann Gordon, who had also been in the Auckland competition, 'You've won,' she said, 'congratulations – I came second.' Victory would, of course, mean more hard work to keep the standards up, but at least Kiri could now see it was worth it.

The following year she returned to Hamilton for the town's own music competition, and won the aria contest. Amongst the finalists in other disciplines was the young New Zealand pianist David Harper who, still in the course of his studies, carried off the concerto prize. Having performed his own work he stayed on in the audience to listen to the singing and thus heard Kiri for the first time. Today David Harper lives in London and is a distinguished singing teacher, coach, and accompanist. He vividly remembers his first encounter with Kiri's voice. 'She sang the "Willow Song" from Verdi's *Otello*, and it was amazing. Her voice was so beautiful I couldn't get over it. That quality we know today was always in it, and she already had enormous flair, a wonderful sense of communication with the audience.'

Back in Auckland after the competition David Harper, while continuing his studies, also began to work with the singers at Sister Mary Leo's music school at St Mary's. He began to accompany Kiri on a fairly regular basis both there and at dinner and rotary singing engagements. He recalls how Kiri 'was already a bit into the life of a grand diva even before she came to England to study. She was like a star: she sang beautifully, looked beautiful – and she was a Maori: Inia Te Wiata was the only other one who'd made it, and he was now in England. Kiri became a myth in her own time in Auckland.' He also recalls that when working with her at St Mary's, 'She wasn't actually lazy, but she used to come into the school in the morning, do a few scales, then go out for a long lunch, come back at about half past two or three o'clock, sing a few songs and go home. Of course, when we were actually rehearsing for a concert she'd work extremely hard, but she had fantastic confidence right from the start – she knew she could just get out there and sing.'

Kiri had two other accompanists, Brooke Monks and Barbara Connelly, both of whom played significant roles in her life. When Kiri sang at nightclubs or made her latest popular recording, it was usually Brooke Monks who was at the piano. Brooke was more than her accompanist – he was also her current boyfriend, indeed virtually her only serious boyfriend until she met Desmond Park in London in 1967, and became his wife in Auckland five months later. Brooke was not a professional musician but the son of a wealthy father who owned a shoe factory, which he has since inherited. Nevertheless he had great talent for what he did at the piano: one has only to listen to those early recordings of 'Maria' and 'Tonight' and to hear his floridly improvised and romantic arpeggios adorning Kiri's exuberantly honeyed singing to appreciate the attraction they must have felt for each other.

David Harper remembers Brooke Monks and a particular occasion when he was called upon to replace him. 'Kiri and Brooke were supposed to be giving a concert in Brooklands Bowl, an enormous open-air arena near New Plymouth. Brooke broke his arm and Ma rang me and asked me to help out by playing for Kiri instead of him. I went over to Ma's place and she fed me up with cakes and made it sound fun. But I was a bit nervous – she wanted me to play the way Brooke did, and I suddenly had to sit down and learn that extravagant style.'

Kiri's other accompanist was made of sterner stuff. Barbara Connelly, or Barbara Brown as she became on marriage, was a New Zealander nine years older than Kiri, who was introduced to her in 1965. The feeling at St Mary's Music School seems to have been that if Kiri were to have someone rather older and more mature working with her, it might concentrate and stabilize her approach to work and thus bring out the full potential of her voice. As Barbara Brown herself puts it: 'I'd just completed my studies in London, was married and had a child, and possessed extremely rigid ideas concerning musical standards and professionalism. Probably because of all that I found myself 'in charge' of this naughty, lovable girl, with all those Maori idiosyncracies that I'd been used to, and which permitted me to smile. I felt that the voice was magnificent, but for some years I wondered whether Kiri would make her fortune from the music I loved or from "Shirley Bassey music" – she could have done either.' Barbara feels that in Maori people 'stickability' is a key word, and that all too few had it. 'But the one thing Kiri did have was her ability to hide her feelings and bounce back fighting fit.' It was 'stickability' that Barbara had to attempt to instil into her young charge. She felt that 'Kiri almost always sang under the note, and this was often caused by her late nights tearing around, and bad planning of practice and study.' She also attributed this fault to her doing 'a great deal of cabaret work – I was sure her flat singing resulted from the type of song chosen for those occasions.'

1965 – the year in which Kiri's twenty-first birthday was duly celebrated in March with an enormous party, to which Nell appeared to have invited most of Auckland – was a watershed. She made her second attempt at the Mobil Song Quest in July. This time it was held in Dunedin, in the south of the South Island – and July down there can be very cold indeed. It was, Kiri already had a cold and the hotel bedroom lacked central heating. But this time urged on by Barbara and with the added responsibility of looking after the youngest contestant, Jackie Champman, who was sharing her room, Kiri avoided the bright lights and social engagements. She sang the 'Habanera' from Bizet's *Carmen* and 'Do not go, my love', and concentrated on singing to the microphone to produce the optimum sound for the judges in the radio studio across town, rather than to the audience sitting in front of her. And this time she won, though the recording today sounds curiously unrelaxed, the voice displaying a heavy, careful mezzo quality which seems unnatural to it. Of all Kiri's early recordings it is possibly the least like her voice as we know it now. Second place in 1965 went to a Dunedin girl, the mezzo soprano Patricia Payne, who a few years later was to become a regular colleague of Kiri's at Covent Garden; another competitor was the young bass Rodney Macann, who was likewise to become a colleague and good friend in England.

After a month of rather sporadic work, driving fast around town on nightclub engagements, and spending a fair amount of her £300 prize money on new dresses to add to her already considerable wardrobe, Kiri set out for Australia with Barbara in September. She had entered her name for the aria competitions of both the *Sydney* and *Melbourne Suns* — sponsored by the respective newspapers and the

[33]

two most prestigious singing prizes in Australasia. The previous year Malvina Major had won at Melbourne, and for Kiri it was vital she should at least equal and if possible surpass, the success of the rival who had pipped her to the post in Hamilton two years before. The prize money from the Mobil Song Quest and from cabaret engagements was helpful for this Australian expedition, as competitors had to meet their own fares and expenses.

Singer and accompanist flew first to the aria contest in Sydney. They stayed with friends of Barbara's, and practised at a local convent where Sister Mary Leo was also staying, in order to hear her protégée compete. The pressure in Australia was commensurately greater than at the competitions in New Zealand and, to make matters worse, Sydney was in the grip of a September heat-wave which frayed tempers and made life even more problematical. In Barbara's view, 'Kiri worked better than she had done at home, but nothing was finished or ready – at St Mary's the final polish had not been put on any of her songs or arias. In fact, when she reached the final she announced to me that she didn't know her second aria, Tosca's "Love and Music". I was horrified and we had to have a recording sent from New Zealand.'

It is fair to say that the dangerous habit of leaving preparations to the last minute has not deserted Kiri. Even today a new operatic role or concert piece will have her exclaiming, 'The performance is next week, and I still don't know it! I'm absolutely not speaking to anybody at all for the next five days!' She will then sit down at home, pull out the score, clap on the headphones, and play the piece over and over again, until it's implanted in her brain. This comes not so much from laziness – once she actually gets down to working at something, there are few singers who apply themselves more intensively – as from her basic attitude to work. Singing for Kiri is emphatically not her 'life', not even her 'career', but simply her 'job', and of course she regards it as her duty to do it as well as she is able. But when she is away from the job and back at home with her family, opera and singing tend to be put aside: opera is not a facet of family life, and is rarely mentioned. Even when there is homework to be done, she finds it all too easy to be distracted by her children, her friends, and the normal daily life of a healthily extrovert young woman who enjoys cooking, entertaining, and playing golf. To work at home means shutting herself away from the people she loves and sees too rarely as it is: so it tends to be put off.

At Sydney, having had a 'dry-run' in front of Sister Mary Leo and the assembled and admiring nuns at the convent in the afternoon, Kiri went on in the extreme heat to the Town Hall for the evening's final. She sang first 'Senza Mamma' – which must have pleased the nuns – from Puccini's *Suor Angelica* (set in a convent) in the first half of the evening, and then in the second 'Ocean, though mighty monster', from Weber's *Oberon* which she says now 'was even more revolting'. Indeed the weariness in her voice was apparent, for she had put all that she had into the Puccini aria earlier in the evening and had left too little in reserve. Nevertheless the audience erupted and stamped and cheered, and on that showing it looked as though Kiri must have won. But the judges decided otherwise, and of the nine finalists she found herself placed equal second, with the prize going to a young Australian of Russian origin, Serge Baigildin. Kiri felt at the time that this really was a slap in the face: second – equal, at that – was not what she had been hoping for. Any amount of rationalization about awarding the prize to a man, or encouraging young immigrants to Australia, did not hide the fact that she had failed to win. Even today it still rankles somewhat, especially as, 'That Russian never got anywhere afterwards – he went to America and was never heard of again.'

She won the critics over, however. The *Sydney Sun* wrote: 'Magnificent soprano Kiri Te Kanawa had the best voice, and showed by far the greatest artistry and acting ability . . . she not only produced a tremendous impact in *Suor Angelica*, but gave as good an account as I have ever heard of Weber's formidable "Ocean" aria.'

Barbara Brown on the other hand, looking back, feels 'It was very much to Kiri's advantage to be pipped to the post – she needed a slap in the face like that to make her think. She'd had a fright; and I moved on the *Melbourne Sun* aria with a quiet, pensive charge.'

[35]

Once there they moved into a convent at Ballarat, a town some miles north-west of the city, and embarked upon a highly disciplined regime of plenty of work, rest, sleep and steak. Barbara recalls, 'At Kiri's suggestion we made rules that no stone would be left unturned. I asked her if she was perfectly sure that was what she wanted. I nagged her about her sleep and diet, and gave her hell during rehearsals. She accepted everything, and I found in my care the most loving and kind young person. Great humility stemmed from her Sydney experience, and a true sense of style and musicianship came from her perseverance and determination through hours of practice and study. A bond was created between us and to this day she is still the most loyal friend.' Barbara's feelings are fully reciprocated by Kiri, who acknowledges today, 'I think Barbara did all this for me because I was a young student and needed help. She did a lot then that I didn't realize at the time. She loved and protected me and was my mother figure at that crucial time.'

The result of such careful preparation was that a far fresher-voiced, better prepared Kiri Te Kanawa sang Agathe's aria 'Leise, leise' – in English as 'Softly sighing' – from Weber's *Der Freischutz*, and – again in English – 'Love and music', the famous 'Vissi d'arte' from the second act of *Tosca*. She says today that she had chosen simpler arias than those she sang in Sydney – but also she unquestionably sang them better and more confidently. The outcome was never in any real doubt, save for Kiri herself: Barbara was well aware that her charge had excelled herself this time, and could now relax. When the judges' decision was announced: 'The first prize goes to New Zealand – to Miss Kiri Te Kanawa', the bouquet dropped from Kiri's hands, which flew up to her face to hide the tears of joy and, above all, of relief. A few moments later a radio microphone was pushed before her to collect an instant reaction. 'Thank you Melbourne, thank you Australia, for letting the prize go to New Zealand' and, finally, 'My heart – it is beating' – worthy of any English translation of an Italian libretto.

The music critic of the *Melbourne Sun*, Linda Phillips, who was one of the two judges, commented after their award: 'The winner has a luscious voice, and a splendid histrionic sense, and therefore would be a splendid actress. She is a very fine opera singer in the making.' The other judge was Stewart Harvey of the Sydney Conservatorium, and his verdict was: 'She had great sincerity in her artistry and will be a great concert performer.' Back at home the *Auckland Star* was jubilant, writing: 'Auckland's Kiri Te Kanawa has swept the *Sun* aria into a bagful of major singing prizes to carry home – this in the land of Melba and Sutherland, remember.'

Kiri's total 'bag' from Australia was the Melbourne prize, worth over £560, a scholarship of over £1300, and the silver laurel aria trophy, plus the Nellie Melba Cup and scholarship, the Star of Opera, the radio vocal and ballad prizes, each worth £100, and the Grand Opera Duet prize, with fellow New Zealander Lynne Cantlon, in Ballarat. It was a rich haul indeed. But after the excitement of victory, the emotional telephone calls home to her parents, and the packed press conference in Melbourne the next morning (which, among many other things, referred to her 'exceptional presence'), Sister Mary Leo's reception upon her return home to Auckland two days later was like the glass of cool, clear water that Kiri was to drink on stage as Arabella in years to come: 'Well, Miss Te Kanawa, back to work again.'

Nevertheless, Auckland itself was only too happy to rejoice. Kiri was met at Whenuapai Airport by a Maori Haka group, along with a crowd of several hundred people, and a couple of nights later sang arias by Bach and Puccini in Auckland Town Hall – sold out of course – accompanied by the Junior Symphony Orchestra. The *New Zealand Herald* the next morning referred to: 'The undisputed queen of song in New Zealand, after her victorious visit across the Tasman', and commented: 'Miss Te Kanawa was at her enchanting best, in spite of some understandable signs of weariness.' The *Auckland Star*'s critic wrote: 'Hers is a magnificent vocal instrument which could carry her as far as she wishes to go. The tone is full and golden, intonation excellent, and visually, of course, she is quite enchanting.' The question that had to be faced now was, where exactly did she wish to go?

[37]

4

England and the London Opera Centre

BOTH NELL TE KANAWA AND SISTER MARY LEO, of course, had been thinking for some time about Kiri's long-term future. Kiri remembers now that back in 1963, when she had been a finalist in the Mobil Song Quest at Hamilton, her parents had been there and had met James Robertson. 'My mother began talking to him. He liked her and she adored him. He told her he had just been appointed Director of the London Opera Centre, and said that if I wanted to go and study there he'd look after me. And he did look after me, very well.' The Sister recalls, 'The suggestion that Kiri should go to study at the London Opera Centre was mine in the first place, as some of my pupils had already undergone training there. Her mother was greatly enthusiastic about this project, and Kiri herself by that time realized that overseas experience was necessary if she was to go further in her singing career.'

In fact, three weeks before Kiri left for Dunedin for her second attempt at the Mobil prize at the end of July 1965, Sister Mary Leo had sent a long, hand-written letter to London, to James Robertson at the Opera Centre. In it she asked for the prospectus and scale of fees to be sent urgently to her, by return, and explained: 'I have a very talented singer in the person of Miss Kiri Te Kanawa, who wishes to further her studies and gain experience abroad.' She reminded Robertson that he had placed her second to Malvina

[38]

Major in the 1963 Mobil Quest, and continued, 'She has improved vastly since and, now only twenty-one, she is considered by musical critics of repute to possess a golden voice of unusual range and quality. Most people (on account of her mellow quality) seem to consider her a mezzo-soprano, but personally I would rather qualify her as a heavy lyric with a mezzo quality: her range is approximately from low G to high C, or D flat.' Observing that general opinion was that Kiri would win first prize at Dunedin, Sister Mary Leo continued, 'At the moment she is much sought after by various concert promoters to perform at musical functions both in Auckland and elsewhere, and the New Zealand Opera Company were most anxious for her to join the company early this year. But I would not consent as I consider her voice has too much potential to allow her to accept a touring contract and be without tuition for six months or more.' She explained that Kiri was going to England with her mother at the end of the year, and, 'While abroad, I would like to place her studies in the hands of some capable person. I feel sure that you will do what you can to advise her in her career, and place her with a suitable coach.' Sister Mary Leo concluded by saying, 'Kiri is a very attractive girl in every way. She is child-like and easily guided, she has a striking personality, good looks and figure. Her parents have left the decision to me as to where to send her. It has been a toss-up between England and America.'

Sister Mary Leo's had not been the only letter to James Robertson. The previous month the Artistic and Musical Director of the New Zealand Opera Company, Dobbs Franks, who had auditioned Kiri shortly before, also wrote, urging him to consider her: 'I suggested to her that she contact you in London for some professional advice as to the proper pursuit of training for her career as a singer . . . She has many physical advantages, such as being young and beautiful.'

Sister Mary Leo's letter took some time to arrive in London, and by the time it was received at the Opera Centre James Robertson had left for his summer holiday. She had signed her letter simply 'S. M. Leo', which prompted Robertson's secretary to reply on

[39]

10 August 1965, 'Dear Sir, Mr Robertson is abroad at present, but meanwhile I am sending you our brochure, together with an application form for Miss Kanawa.' This letter was addressed to Mr S. M. Leo at St Mary's School of Music.

Only two days later James Robertson himself wrote to Sister Mary Leo. He began by saying, 'My secretary apologizes for having addressed you as a man – but there was no way in which she could have realized that St Mary's School of Music was part of à convent.' More to the point, he continued, 'I remember Kiri Te Kanawa very vividly, and I have no doubt at all that she would be acceptable as a student at the London Opera Centre. Incidentally, Mr Dobbs Franks has already written to me on her behalf. She thus has three strong recommendations – yours, his and mine – so that we shall accept her without audition.'

Kiri meanwhile had received the application form, filled it in and returned it to London. Endorsed by James Robertson 'Should be accepted without audition' in the top right-hand corner, it still lies in the now-defunct Opera Centre's files at the offices of the Arts Council in London. On it she gave her nationality as quarter Maori/European, her height as 5 ft 6½ins, her weight as ten stone, and her voice as mezzo-soprano. She stated her qualifications as two years' secondary education at St Mary's, one year at Auckland Business College, ATCL Honours, and Royal Grade 8 Distinction in music, and Grade 6 Distinction in Theory. Under experience she listed: 'Six years in Sister Mary Leo's School of Music Choir, concerts with orchestra, radio, television and film work, various local operatic and musical comedy performances, recordings.' She added under this head: 'John Court Aria Prize, Mobil Song Quest, and every major prize offered for competition in New Zealand.' It was a fair summary of achievement for a girl only just over twenty-one.

Kiri herself was only slightly doubtful about leaving for England. 'I had Brooke to love, friends to love, and life was good for me in New Zealand. But I knew that I needed another country if I was to advance myself. New Zealand is either for the very young or the very old, and I was at the beginning of my intermediate period, and I knew I had something more to accomplish. It wasn't that I had a driving desire to be great or anything, just that I knew my life was not to be staying around Auckland being lazy, probably getting married and having children. Being adopted, as I had been, makes you a survivor, as did my mother, who was ambitious for me and a real tryer. She had decided I should leave, and of course I was convinced by her and quite agreed that I had to.' Kiri admits today to having loved Brooke very much, but concedes that he lacked the practicality she was to find in her husband, Desmond. Nevertheless, when she left for England in 1966 she was 'unofficially engaged' to Brooke, and remained that way until the summer of the following year, when she took the plunge and decided to marry Desmond instead. Had Kiri married Brooke Monks it would almost certainly have meant a New Zealand-based, probably carefree, possibly relatively successful life – but never the career of the top class international opera singer.

In fact their actual departure did not take place until early 1966 as there was so much that had to be done first. Shortly after Kiri's return from Australia came an invitation to make a trip with Barbara Connelly to Los Angeles as guests of the Douglas Aircraft Corporation, to celebrate Air New Zealand's inaugural direct jet flight between Auckland and California. All Kiri was required to do was to sing at the celebratory banquet when she arrived and, needless to say, the invitation was eagerly accepted. She remembers it now as 'A foolish trip: as soon as I arrived in Honolulu they said "Come and sing", so foolish Kiri, with jet lag, went and sang. Then we went on to Los Angeles where we were pampered, ran into another Maori girl who ferried us round and wined and dined us, and we were totally spoiled and I came home on Cloud Nine.' The trip may have been free, but nevertheless proved costly in terms of presents bought for her parents and the dresses and souvenirs that Kiri found irresistible in Los Angeles shops. Still, it did have the advantage of confirming her liking for overseas travel and thus hardening her determination to leave for England.

Once back from Los Angeles money, for the first time, began

to play a really significant role in her life. If she were to go to study in England she would have to find a way both of paying the fees and of supporting herself, for the London Opera Centre was not in a position to offer her a scholarship and her parents still had very little to spare. It was true that she was by now enjoying some regular income from her recordings, which were becoming ever more popular with the New Zealand public – she even won a golden disc – she had some television work and was featured in a couple of New Zealand-made films. But the fact remained that she had insufficient funds for three years of life and study in England, where she would most probably be earning nothing at all. In the end the Queen Elizabeth II Arts Council of New Zealand was bullied and cajoled, largely by an eighty-six-year-old concert promoter named Gladstone Hill, into offering assistance, and a Foundation Scholarship was set up for Kiri's trip. Kiri describes Hill as 'A very wonderful old man, who managed to persuade the government to help me; yet another person I can never forget.' The arrangement was that the New Zealand Arts Council agreed to match the sum that Kiri herself could produce for her stay in England. This turned out to be (slightly to her surprise in view of the rate at which she spent money) £2500. So, when she left for England at the beginning of 1966, it was with £5000 which, she says now, 'was more than any student deserved'. She also left with 'all my household belongings, pots and pans, and six or eight trunks full of clothes'.

First, however, New Zealanders wanted to say goodbye to their home-grown star, and a series of six farewell concerts were organized in the three months before her departure culminating, two days before the ship sailed, with one in the capital city, Wellington. The town hall holds two thousand people and had been sold out well in advance. Raewyn Blade was among those lucky enough to get a seat and remembers, 'I was in floods of tears, like everyone else there. The next time I wept like that was ten years later when I heard her sing Desdemona in Verdi's *Otello* at Covent Garden: I'd heard her sing it when she won the John Court Aria in Auckland a decade earlier, and it just seemed unbelievable that now she was

up there on stage at the Royal Opera House – the star of the show.'
At these concerts Kiri gave her admirers a selection of all her work:
operatic arias, popular songs, Maori folksongs, and at Wellington,
for her final encore, that traditional and inimitable Maori song of
farewell 'Now is the hour'. When Gladstone Hill finally stood up to
make a speech wishing her well he broke down; of course – it was
that kind of occasion.

Back at home in Blockhouse Bay the next day came her family
farewell. Nell had organized a garden party for about three hundred
of Kiri's friends. David Harper was there and reflects, 'By then
Kiri was just queen of the place, an amazing voice that was going
to go to the top. And Ma was always behind her: an incredible
woman – she could have been a star in public relations but devoted
it all to her daughter.' As a leaving present from her father, who was
going to stay behind getting on with his job, Kiri received something
very special: an oblong pendant of New Zealand greenstone, a
Whakakai, representing a small fish, the symbol of the Te Kanawas.
Her uncle, Mita, had worn it as he fought through the Second World
War, and Kiri wears it round her neck to this day.

A few days earlier perhaps Kiri's most moving adieu had taken
place when she went to a dinner in Te Kuiti given in her honour by
her Maori relatives. With her uncle Shine she visited the legendary
ancestral cave in the family's Hangatiki Limeworks. Previously
another Maori relative, Rotokiki Jones, had told once again the
famous story of the Te Kanawa chief meeting the fairy in the cave,
but now uncle Mita spoke rather more seriously. 'Kiri, we knew you
were good and you would go at least halfway. But now that you've
been here and done everything you should, we know that you'll go
all the way. Now I am very happy – this makes us all very happy.'
Kiri's reply was to pick up a small piece of limestone from the floor
of the cave and put it in her bag. At least some part of New Zealand
and her Maori ancestors would accompany her to Britain.

She was seen off by hundreds of friends and well-wishers who
sang 'Now is the hour' on the quayside as the *Australia* pulled out of
Auckland harbour. The ship's owners, Chandris Lines, had offered

a free passage in return for Kiri singing at a concert on board. She had met nobody in particular during the three week voyage, and knew very few people in London. Kiri and Nell, with all their cabin trunks, arrived in London on her twenty-second birthday – 6 March 1966. Initially they moved into a flat in Richmond which New Zealand acquaintances were vacating, but Kiri quickly discovered that even by car it would take at least an hour and a half to travel from there to the Opera Centre in the East End of London. So they found a reasonably spacious basement flat in Forest Hill – between Catford and Dulwich – which, although south of the river and not exactly next door to the Opera Centre in dockland, was a more manageable journey. To help with the travelling she bought a large second-hand Ford car, and swiftly acquired a taxi-driver's knowledge of London back-streets and short-cuts which she retains to this day, making her a disconcertingly critical passenger should one be driving her anywhere.

The spring term had already begun at the London Opera Centre so, at James Robertson's suggestion, she went along as an observer for the final four weeks before the Easter holidays. Then she immediately took a wholly unnecessary holiday to Paris and Italy ('just to have a quick look round') before starting her first full term as a student at the LOC. The Centre was housed in a cavernous former cinema called The Troxy in the Commercial Road, about two miles east of the City. It is not a welcoming place, and the large photographic blow-ups of well-known opera singers in mainly Wagnerian costume did little to hide its cinematic origins, or makeshift conversion. Although the London Opera Centre itself closed down a few years ago, the building remains the Royal Opera's main rehearsal studio until the new extension to the Opera House opens in Covent Garden. Kiri has thus continued to travel down the Commercial Road to it throughout her career, and preserved the total dislike she felt for the building ever since she first entered it. Each Covent Garden production she rehearses there now she vows will be her last, and every malady, actual or imaginary, is attributed to 'that dreadful, airless place'. One can understand her deep-rooted loathing for such a gloomy, uninspiring edifice – particularly being so used to the outdoor life of New Zealand. Nor was she helped by the fact that initially the only people working there whom she knew were James Robertson himself, and Malvina Major, her old rival from New Zealand, now married and in her second year at the Centre. Kiri felt very lonely.

She remains quite frank about her initial and continuing unhappiness at the Opera Centre. Aside from anything else she had been, in New Zealand, a free agent and, more than that, a celebrity who was almost universally loved and admired. Apart from her work with Sister Mary Leo she had never previously been a formal music student anywhere. Now, in London, she was a total unknown who, at the relatively late age of twenty-two, was just about to start full-time study for the first time· in her life. 'It was strange to see everyone taking life so seriously, when I was having such a ball. They told me I didn't take it seriously enough and I replied that it wasn't my life and death. They weren't going to take my blood and ruin my life, and if I wanted to go to a movie or a party, I'd go. I wasn't going to be caged in by things called "study", "music lessons", and "homework". The trouble was that they already knew the system, whilst I couldn't bring myself to read the schedule for three months. I was totally miserable for one whole year and nobody seemed to want to help. I suddenly realized that I was in the big bad world and I didn't know whether I was going to win or lose: I didn't really feel at that point I was going to win very much.'

Another major problem was that of relations with her mother. Their two strongly extrovert personalities used to clash often enough at home in Auckland, but those quarrels invariably ended in laughter: there was always plenty happening in New Zealand to relieve the tension and Nell had ample opportunity to consume her abundant energy in organizing her daughter's career. In London it was a different story: like Kiri, she was a stranger there who knew almost nobody, and while her daughter spent her days at the Opera Centre she was left with virtually nothing to do. The result was that when Kiri was at the flat the quarrels became more frequent, more bitter, and longer-lasting than before. The situation was to some extent eased by the arrival in London of Kiri's friend from Auckland, Raewyn Blade, who had come to study singing and acting at Guildhall School. She had found a flat she hated and rang Kiri to tell her that mushrooms were growing on the wall. 'Come and share my mushrooms instead!' was the reply, and Raewyn promptly moved in.

For all her great success at home in New Zealand, Kiri had always remained very much Nell's adored youngest daughter, who needed constant protection. Indeed, until she left for the *Sydney Sun* aria competition in 1965, she had never been further away from home on her own than the South Island. Home life in Blockhouse Bay had always been paramount, and it was only when Kiri arrived in London that, at the relatively late age of twenty-two, she really began to feel herself an adult person, independent of her mother and father. It was hardly surprising that, once at the Opera Centre, among fellow students who had been leading independent lives for some time and some of whom were already married, she should begin to resist and resent the constant presence and pressure of her mother. Equally, in the circumstances of their life so far, it was even less surprising that Nell should resist her daughter's efforts finally to untie the apron strings.

Not long after Raewyn's arrival, Nell decided to go home to New Zealand and Kiri now admits, 'She was broken-hearted that I sent her away. But I said, 'Mummy, you've got to go – we're not getting on and your life is a misery. Daddy needs you at home more than I do here.' It wasn't that she was cramping my style – there was no style to cramp. But I'd suddenly tasted freedom and wanted to be able to stay out late if I felt like it. She loved me dearly, I know, and when she went home she said she'd forgiven me but that I'd hurt her a lot. All I could say was, 'Well, Mummy, that's the way with children – I'm sure one day my daughter will do it to me.''

Such domestic problems were doing little to help Kiri's work at the Opera Centre where several of her fellow students, such as Josephine Barstow, Malvina Major, Deirdre Pleydell, Alexandra, formerly Ann, Gordon and the Australian tenor Donald Smith's son, Robin Donald, were beginning to make solid and substantial progress. Many of Kiri's teachers were beginning to lose patience with her apparent lack of application, and it was even being suggested that James Robertson had made a mistake in accepting her in the first place. Fortunately, there was one person there who did manage to penetrate Kiri's sense of isolation and proved capable of under-standing her. This was June Megennis, now June Hall, an attractive blonde girl, much the same age as Kiri, who was James Robertson's personal assistant.

June Hall found, 'She was a gawky schoolgirl-type then, but in New Zealand she'd obviously been a celebrity: she'd had more or less everything she wanted and was almost a star there. Coming to the Opera Centre and having to fit in with thirty-five or forty others made it difficult for her to adjust. She already had a beautiful face, but she wasn't very elegant – rather tomboyish and a bit overweight.' June's became the shoulder for Kiri to cry on when, as frequently happened, she fell behind with her studies and irritated her teachers. 'She knew she could come to me on the days when things had gone badly. She couldn't apply herself to German or Italian, for example, and it was really traumatic for her. She'd come into my office in tears and say she couldn't face it again, and that she wanted to run away. Then the next day she wouldn't come in to the Centre at all and I'd have to ring her up and say this isn't the way to behave. The trouble was she didn't have any friends among the students, and though the teachers were marvellous they weren't really sympathetic to her. They expected students to learn parts quickly, and for Kiri even learning the music was difficult – she'd had no previous formal training at all. She could learn the notes but found interpretation very hard. Most of the other students were post-graduate and quite used to learning, and Kiri was having to take her classes with them, so it showed her up.

'James was under a lot of pressure from teachers who wouldn't give her parts as they didn't think she was serious enough about it. They didn't understand her as a person or the problems she was

[47]

having, and thought she was just fooling about because she was a rich girl with lots of clothes and a good voice who had been earning good money in New Zealand while others were still on grants. I remember one of the Sadler's Wells Opera's producers, John Blatchley, used to come to the Centre to give coaching and produce end of term workshops. He despaired of Kiri and said he thought we were wasting our time – she was never going to get anywhere. I told him there and then I was quite sure she was going to make it, and I bet him £50 she would – John still owes me the money!'

The reason for June's confidence in Kiri was that she had already noticed, as some others had failed to do, how great was her own basic confidence in her voice, and how much she loved and responded to an audience: when Kiri was performing on stage, in public, her uncertainty vanished, and she instinctively knew how to sing at her best and how to move around a stage. Wherever and whatever she is performing, in opera house or concert hall, Kiri radiates this sheer joy of singing, and enormous confidence and relaxation. The effect on the audience is dramatic: each member feels that she is singing specially for him or her, and that this is a particularly special performance. It is this instinctive ability to respond to the music and to the audience that has been the foundation of her success, and the reason that audiences so adore her and flock to hear her.

5

Desmond

LIFE IN LONDON was not entirely gloomy for Kiri, however. At Forest Hill the flat, since Nell's departure was proving a great success. Things became even better when Sally Rush (now Sally Sloman) arrived in London from New Zealand on an extended working holiday. She contacted Kiri, who invited her to come and use the spare bed: she stayed for several months before returning to New Zealand. Looking back on them, Raewyn has many happy memories of their student days in Forest Hill. 'For example there was the night I came back late from Guildhall and went to have a bath. The bathroom was in the basement, and I was warbling away when suddenly I saw a pair of eyes staring in through the window. I hit the traditional top C, and Kiri came storming in like a herd of buffaloes, flung open the front door and chased after a little man in a mackintosh, screaming at the top of her voice. We didn't catch him so we called the police who, when they found three young New Zealand girls sharing a flat, gave us their full-time protection for the next three months.'

Police protection led to police parties, and then to an invitation to spend the weekend at a cottage in Oxfordshire with some of the young officers; they were just a little disappointed when the three girls climbed into the cottage's only bed together, leaving their hosts to sleep on the floor. Raewyn recalls another party, this time given by some young lawyers in Chelsea. 'We didn't know anyone and a young chap came over to us and said, "Excuse me, I believe you're both New Zealanders – are New Zealand girls all as tall and strong as you are?" "Yes," said Kiri, looking down his tie, "but you should see the men." We weren't asked back.'

Another connection between Kiri and the police was established through June at the Opera Centre, who was by now engaged to a young detective constable in the Port of London Police called David Hall. His chief inspector, now chief constable of the Port of London, was Jim Tuplin and he used to organize the annual parties given by the CID. Originally these had been 'stag nights', but Tuplin decided they might be more fun as 'mixed' evenings and that it might even be worth trying to introduce a little culture. Through David Hall, June's help was sought in discovering whether any students at the Opera Centre might be willing to sing for them, and Kiri was only too happy to perform for an appreciative audience. She did so several times, giving them a mixture of operatic arias and her previous New Zealand club repertoire, which proved just as popular in London's dockland. Both Jim Tuplin and June still remember the night at the West India Dock Police Club when, in a room full of smoke, alcohol, police officers and their wives and guests, accompanied by an out-of-tune piano, Kiri suddenly stood up and sang the Lord's Prayer – the effect was such that one could have heard a pin drop. Jim Tuplin was in charge of funds and so had to pay the performers. The first occasion he gave Kiri a bottle of whisky – on the second it was at least two bottles, as she was so very popular.

Another vocal engagement under police auspices was to have more lasting consequences. On 4 March 1967 June and David Hall were married; Kiri was a guest and was invited to sing at the end of the marriage service, though June did not actually hear her as she and her husband were signing the register at the time. The reception afterwards was given at the Opera Centre; Kiri went to that too and drank a good deal of champagne before going out for the evening on a blind date. 'Raewyn had told me about an absolutely gorgeous blond Australian mining engineer. He'd come over on a boat with Bill Double, a photographer whom Sally knew and who had taken photos of me in New Zealand, and a third man called David Barr would be with them. We all met at Piccadilly Circus, outside Swan and Edgar, and then went to see a film *Night of the Generals*, which I remember wasn't any good. Then afterwards we all attempted to find our way back to my car, and got separated as I'd forgotten where I'd parked it! Rae and David Barr got lost and never came back, but the other four of us eventually returned to Forest Hill to have a cup of coffee, and then the boys stayed the night. But we were all very proper – there were four beds! It had been a good evening and, as it turned out, I'd found my Mr Ideal – he was called Desmond Park.'

Desmond had been born in Brisbane in Queensland on the east coast of Australia on 20 July 1942, making him by then just short of twenty-five – nearly two years older than Kiri. His father was a businessman – amongst whose accomplishments was the ability to tune pianos. He and his wife used regularly to take Desmond to performances of Gilbert and Sullivan, amongst other things, at His Majesty's Theatre in Brisbane. But despite that, Desmond had no great enthusiasm for music, and at the University of Queensland he had taken a degree in engineering. From university he took a job with a mining firm at their copper refining plant at Townsville, up the coast from Brisbane. He then decided, like a lot of Australians, to go to England on the normal 'extended holiday'. His company in Australia had organized a job for him with their subsidiary in England, the Britannia Lead Company at Gravesend in Kent. But the job didn't work out very well, and during his visit Desmond arranged an aviation job in America at Rockford, Illinois. He was due to leave England at the end of 1967 – if Kiri had not appeared on the scene.

On the boat coming to England, Des and his Italian-Australian friend, Franco Pieri, had met the New Zealand photographer Bill Double. Bill planned to live in Cranley Gardens, South Kensington, and Desmond was living in Meopham in Kent to be near his work, so the Double flat became his London base. Desmond recalls being telephoned by Double and asked to make up the six on that evening out at the cinema, but has little detailed memory of the evening itself, nor did meeting Kiri for the first time leave any great impression on him, save that of a good-looking, good-natured girl. Her name, to a non-musical Australian, had meant nothing at all; he remembers, 'As a student at some place called the London Opera Centre, her main objective of student life seemed to be to get away from it. She seemed keen on making a career in music, but not so keen on applying herself. After that first evening I don't think we made contact again for about a month, and I can't remember now exactly why I did phone her again.'

For Kiri her first meeting with Desmond had sounded a rather different note. She had just spent Christmas at home in New Zealand, against the wishes of the Opera Centre, and whilst there had seen a good deal of Brooke Monks. By the time she left she felt it was highly likely that she would complete another year at the Opera Centre, then return to New Zealand for ever and marry Brooke. Her initial meeting with Desmond was far from being a case of love at first sight, but he did strike her at once as a polite, polished and well-educated young man, who had all the qualities that might make him suitable for a lasting relationship. It was a fair assessment: as she says now, 'For fifteen years we've been good buddies, and that's surely what being married is all about.'

When Desmond did telephone to arrange a second meeting he was lucky to find Kiri at Forest Hill: she was about to move house, a move that had come about through one of those happy chances that seem to characterize the lives of the successful. Veronica Haigh had arrived on the scene. She was an unmarried, middle-aged Englishwoman who came from a wealthy and artistic family. She was a writer, painter and actress, and had been passionately interested in New Zealand, particularly in the Maoris, since her childhood. She has even written an opera (music and libretto) about a Maori folk-myth *Totara Bay*, which it is her dream to see performed at Covent Garden with Kiri in the title role. Miss Haigh had been in New

Zealand, with the Royal Shakespeare Company, in 1963, and had heard a record of Kiri singing the 'Nuns' Chorus' from *Casanova*; she was instantly struck by the beauty of her voice. Back in London in 1967 she had discovered that Kiri was now there too, studying at the Opera Centre and living in Forest Hill. Veronica Haigh herself owned a beautiful and spacious old mews house (once part of the stables of Kensington Palace) in De Vere Gardens, off Kensington Road near the Albert Hall, in which she lived when she was in London and not on her antipodean travels. She decided this would be a far more suitable place for Kiri to live than in Forest Hill, and that she would be able to enjoy a more settled life there. Accordingly she telephoned Kiri, introduced herself, and invited her to De Vere Gardens for dinner. Miss Haigh recalls Kiri instantly liking the house, so she asked her to come and live there. Having established that she could bring Raewyn too, Kiri quickly agreed. She found it, 'A large old house on four floors with an attic: very beautiful, but in rather a bad state of repair; and Veronica Haigh was very kind, above all in charging only a minimal rent.' Raewyn recalls she had gone to Paris for an Easter break in 1967, having told Kiri that she had had enough of Forest Hill and would be moving out on her return. When she came back it was her birthday; when Raewyn arrived at Forest Hill Kiri's words were, 'Come in, Rae – happy birthday – we're having a quick party, then we're moving out tomorrow!'

Desmond was at the party, helped them to move the following day and from then on began to see Kiri regularly. He would come up to London from Gravesend on a Saturday and would stay the weekend at De Vere Gardens though, as Kiri recalls, 'It was all perfectly above board – Mummy would have been proud of me!' After a few weeks, however, there came a time when Kiri decided not to see him one weekend, and got somebody in the house to answer the telephone and say she was not there. The result was that an enormous bunch of flowers arrived, with a card saying 'Love, Desmond' – though he told Kiri later he had originally written a goodbye message to accompany the flowers, but had had second thoughts at the last moment. Additionally unsettling was the presence of an old boy-friend from New Zealand, the bass Rodney Macann; he was now in London and was also coming to De Vere Gardens and showing great interest in Kiri. She told him, however, that he was two years too late: in New Zealand two years earlier she had loved him very much, but things had now changed.

A milestone was reached during a boating weekend on the Thames with some of Desmond's Australian friends. Kiri hesitated about going and delayed their departure so that she and Desmond arrived half a day late. But once on the boat she found that, 'Suddenly the fresh air, jeans, T-shirts, and sun changed my whole attitude, and I thought, "To hell with it – goodbye Brooke!"' It was as well she had come to a decision: she was due to return to New Zealand during the Opera Centre's summer vacation – some concerts had been arranged to supplement her income from her grant – and Brooke had already started a series of increasingly insistent telephone calls from Auckland.

Desmond had by now suggested that they should try living together, but Kiri informed him that she was returning to New Zealand to try to sort things out. He told her that when she got back it would have to be just the two of them; to which Kiri replied that if that meant they were going to get married, perhaps they had better get engaged first. So Desmond went out and bought her an engagement ring, which she still wears and treasures, then went off on his planned holiday to Italy with Franco Pieri, having arranged to telephone Kiri in New Zealand to find out her parents' reaction to their engagement. He also wrote formally to the Te Kanawas.

Kiri flew out to Auckland a few days later, and by chance met Raewyn's parents on the plane. They had heard that she was engaged – and discovered with relief that it was not to Brooke. When Brooke telephoned her she told him she was going to marry a man she had met in London, called Desmond Park. 'He was furious,' says Kiri, 'basically because he didn't ask first.' Her mother's reaction was somewhat different. 'I remember both my parents were very quiet in the car coming home from the airport. Mummy said she'd received the letter and asked me when I wanted to get married.

I told her "straight away" and she asked why I was so eager. I suddenly realized she was convinced I was pregnant and that once again I'd destroyed her life and wrecked her dreams. Anyway she took it in her stride, and with three weeks had us married in Auckland. Even though I'd said "Straight away", I'd planned to go back to London and do it quietly there, but Mummy wanted the full bit – and got it.'

Accordingly when Desmond telephoned from a village call-box in the middle of Italy he was greeted with the news that they were getting married in Auckland in less than a week's time. He took a train to Rome and, using the money his father had sent him to go to America, bought an air ticket to New Zealand via Brisbane instead. On his arrival at Brisbane airport he telephoned his parents with the news – his father promptly took ill, so they were unable to come to the wedding – but Desmond managed to pick up a couple of 'best men' (Adolf Lacis and James Love) and flew on to Auckland. He says now, 'It was a great shock to me when I got to Auckland airport, pitched off the plane and found a newspaper photographer waiting to take my photograph. I hadn't appreciated that Kiri was really so well known there. Though Bill Double had tried to warn me, it hadn't seemed so significant in England. But the day after my arrival I found myself on the front page of the *Auckland Star* and other New Zealand papers, and that evening the television cameras came to the Te Kanawa household and we were on the national news.'

Kiri and Desmond were married in St Patrick's Roman Catholic Cathedral, Auckland on Wednesday, 30 August 1967 – but four days earlier there had been an important musical engagement. At the town hall in Wellington – scene of that highly emotional farewell concert eighteen months earlier – Kiri, now billed 'Queen of Song' gave a massive recital. She was accompanied by her old friend David Harper; he was due to leave immediately after her wedding for the Royal College of Music in London to pursue his studies as the next holder, after Kiri, of a Queen Elizabeth Arts Council Scholarship. The concert had been organized once again by Gladstone Hill, the man who had done so much to support her move to London, and it

[55]

was under the auspices of the Kiri Te Kanawa Trust Board which had been set up to supervise the funds which had been collected to support her in Britain. The chairman of the Trust, H. J. (Bill) Barrett, General Manager of the Auckland Savings Bank and old friend of the Te Kanawas, had also undertaken the arrangements for the wedding in Auckland.

The souvenir programme for this concert is a vivid illustration of precisely how great a New Zealand celebrity Desmond Park was marrying. It included letters to Gladstone Hill from Sir Walter Nash, who had been New Zealand's Prime Minister from 1957–60 and from Ralph Hanan, Attorney General and Minister for Maori Affairs in Keith Holyoake's government which had replaced the Nash administration. Sir Walter's letter concluded: 'Kiri Te Kanawa has given, and will give through the years, the wisdom, courage and joy inherent in the qualities of her people.' The Minister wrote: 'I can think of no better representative of the Maori people and of all New Zealand than Kiri . . . it is my sincere hope that she will reach the top and be acclaimed "Diva", a great woman singer. But, however bright her future, we know that she will always remain in our thoughts as Kiri, the gracious, charming girl who captured the hearts of the New Zealand people.'

From a girl with other matters on her mind one might have expected an easy-going, undemanding programme on this occasion – but Kiri is not that sort of girl and proudly unleashed her full repertory upon the Wellington audience – the hall had been sold out two months before. She opened with Dido's 'Lament' from Purcell's opera *Dido and Aeneas*, which she had sung with London Opera Centre during the year, both at Caen in Normandy and at the Purcell Room, part of the Royal Festival Hall complex on London's South Bank. Alan Blyth, now music critic of the *Daily Telegraph,* had covered that concert for the *Daily Express*, and the Wellington programme reprinted his comments: 'Trying to spot the next decade's operatic star is nearly as difficult as picking a winner on the racecourse – and just as intriguing . . . If I had to put my money on it, I would back a magnetic twenty-three-year-old soprano called Kiri

Te Kanawa from New Zealand . . . Miss Te Kanawa sang with a full, perfectly focussed tone as the ill-fated Queen Dido in Purcell's opera, suggesting that she is now ready for employment in any opera house you care to name.' Writing on 22 June 1967, Mr Blyth showed prescience indeed.

After this weighty opening Kiri reminded the audience of her earlier triumphs in Mobil Song Quests and other New Zealand competitions with three of her early favourites: 'The Tryst' by Sibelius, Frank Bridge's 'Love Went A-Riding', and Richard Hageman's 'Do Not Go, My Love'. After solo piano pieces from David Harper came Musetta's 'Waltz Song' from Puccini's *La Bohème,* the slave-girl Liu's two arias from that composer's *Turandot,* and Marguerite's 'Jewel Song' from Gounod's *Faust.* After the interval she sang 'Vissi d'arte', Tosca's great second act aria, Madam Butterfly's 'One fine day' and the 'Habanera' and 'Seguidilla' from Bizet's *Carmen,* a role she was to sing with Northern Opera in Newcastle-upon-Tyne the following April, and back in New Zealand in 1969. Her final group contained 'They call me Mimi' from *La Bohème,* Rosina's 'Una voce poco fa' from *The Barber of Seville,* and finally 'Doretta's Dream' from Puccini's *La Rondine* (which is also the latest complete opera recording that Kiri has made, at the end of 1981). It was a colossal programme and at times the strain showed; nevertheless, she added a Bach air as an encore before singing the Maori folk-song without which no New Zealand audience would ever allow her to leave the platform.

Her wedding four days later is still vividly remembered in New Zealand – at the time it had seemed almost a State occasion. There was extensive press coverage and the New Zealand *Woman's Weekly,* in its issue of 11 September, had Kiri and Desmond on the cover, cutting their cake, a special colour feature inside and dubbed her 'Bride of the Year'. Sally Rush, her flat-mate in Forest Hill, was now back nursing in Auckland; Kiri asked her to be chief bridesmaid, along with two of her other friends, the singer Lindsay Kearns, and Nan Taylor. Sally recalls: 'Wedding fever hit Auckland. I had been staying at Kiri's home for the previous two days, and the day before the wedding Ma and I had rung Auckland's Traffic Department to suggest that there might be a few onlookers who could cause traffic problems. They laughingly dismissed that as nonsense and reluctantly provided only five officers to control over two thousand well-wishers who thronged the church the next day.'

Although the service at St Patrick's Cathedral was not until two in the afternoon, Betty Hanson remembers going down there in the morning to find 'hundreds of little old ladies with their picnic boxes already on the pavement, staking their claims', and later her son Robert had to 'fight a way through old ladies with handbags to get into the church'. Despite Nell Te Kanawa's considerable organizational powers, combined with those of Bill Barrett, the whole affair was being arranged at such short notice that traumas were inevitable. Sally and Kiri, for example, stayed in bed quite late that morning and decided to ring the local radio station with a 'request' for Desmond – the announcer played 'Don't Sleep in the Subway, Darling'. Then suddenly they realized that they should visit the hairdresser, and in a panic made urgent appointments and dashed into town. Once there Sally realized it was not simply a question of having their hair done, but of kneeling on the floor and making netted snoods for the bridesmaids, while her sister Mary, who was a floral artist, organized the flowers that Kiri had insisted on putting in their hair.

Despite all the last-minute hitches – perhaps because of them – and despite the huge crowd causing Kiri to arrive late and tearful at the church, the wedding went magnificently. Kiri's dress was a striking off-white silk shantung creation in medieval style, made by a well-known Auckland dress designer, Colin Cole. She wore a pill-box hat with conical peak – again operatic and medieval – from which hung her veil, and a long train fell from her shoulders: she looked superb. Nell had invited some three hundred guests, among them the Maori Queen Te-Ata-i-rangi-kaahu and her husband Mr Te Whatu Moana, other prominent Maoris, and the Mayor and Mayoress of Auckland. A Maori priest, Father Tate, conducted the marriage service, which had no nuptial mass as Desmond is a Protestant. Needless to say, Sister Mary Leo was also there, con-

[58]

ducting her choir as Kiri walked up the aisle. She, too, had had difficulty getting to the church on time, as Sally Rush's brother, guarding a side door, had to be convinced before he would let her in that she was not an interloper. Along with Adolf Lacis and James Love, Robert Hanson was a groomsman and the ten ushers included four of his brothers. Also among the ushers were Lou Clausen and Simon Mihana – the famous duo of Lou and Simon with whom Kiri had sung in her pre-London days.

After the service and even greater difficulty in leaving the church ('pandemonium reigned' according to the *Woman's Weekly* and reminded Sergeant Williams of the Auckland City Traffic department of the 1956 Springbok Test at Eden Park) a huge reception was held in Trillo's Restaurant at Westhaven on Auckland harbour. Kiri had sung there frequently during her cabaret career and its owner, Cliff Trillo, had always promised that he would hold her wedding reception when the day came. For Desmond, already overwhelmed, it was 'The best party I have been to in my life. There was an enormous soup tureen full of oysters, masses of Great Western champagne – including my two personal bottles – and whenever my best man said "Another scotch" I thought he meant a bottle – when in fact he was talking about a case. I sang in public for the first, and only, time in my life – "Waltzing Matilda", of course! It cost us a fortune and we were stony broke afterwards: Nell was determined to have a big splurge but there was no way in which she and Tom were going to be able to pay for it all, so Kiri and I had to pitch in too.' Nell's reaction was to tell the *Woman's Weekly*: 'Everything has gone so fast in the last three weeks, I wish I could have the wedding all over again.'

For their honeymoon Kiri and Desmond went first to the hot springs of Taupo, and then on for a week's skiing where, says Kiri, 'We were always last up the mountain and first down.' On their way back to England they flew to Brisbane so that Kiri could meet her husband's parents; they got on splendidly. 'They are lovely people – they've taken me as their daughter and that's it.' But their stay in Brisbane had to be a short one – Kiri was due back at the Opera

[59]

Centre for the new term and Desmond, who had left his company in Gravesend before the holiday in Italy, had to find a job. But marriage was to prove a great step forward for both of them: and from now on Kiri's life was to take a steadier and even more successful course.

6

First London Successes

Despite her difficulties and unhappiness there, Kiri had been able to make some degree of progress at the Opera Centre up to the time she left for New Zealand in August 1967. In addition to classes, coaching and master classes there, she had also found a personal singing teacher with whom she was getting on well and who was improving her technique and increasing her self-confidence. Originally, shortly after her arrival at the Centre in 1966, Kiri had been recommended to Margaret Krauss, a German lady who had previously taught in Sydney where she had seen Kiri compete in the *Sun* aria competition the year before. She was the singing teacher of the well-known mezzo-soprano Margreta Elkins and gave lessons at London's Wigmore Hall. Kiri started to take lessons with her, but sadly the relationship did not flourish. She found herself gaining very little confidence; Miss Krauss's lessons left her with the feeling that she had little future as a singer. Mary Masterton, a fellow New Zealander studying in London, recommended Kiri to another teacher, Florence Norberg, a Norwegian who taught in her flat in George Street, Marylebone and who had popular, as well as operatic, singers among her pupils. Kiri liked her immensely and spent two happy years with Miss Norberg until after she had left the Opera Centre and was auditioning for Covent Garden.

Early on in her days at the Opera Centre, in 1966, Kiri had attended a master class given by Joan Sutherland's husband, the conductor Richard Bonynge, at which the great Australian soprano had also been present. Despite fear and trepidation at the august audience, Kiri had managed to sing for him and had impressed them both. Having listened carefully to her voice, Bonynge expressed the view that she was not a mezzo-soprano at all and would be far better employed tackling the soprano repertory. For Kiri this was not unlike the word of God: 'I'd have believed him if he'd said I was a contralto!' Up to that point the roles she had worked on at the Centre – Dorabella in Mozart's *Così fan tutte*, and Vera Boronel in Menotti's *The Consul*, with Josephine Barstow in the leading role of Magda – had both been mezzo parts. But James Robertson and the teachers at the Centre took note of what Richard Bonynge said and began gradually to expand her range upwards.

Meanwhile, during the rest of 1966, she sang two other roles in little-known operas in performances at the Opera Centre. The first of these was the 'trouser role' of the Marquis de Bluette in Delibes' seldom heard *Le Roi l'a dit*, in which Josephine Barstow also played a male role. Then at the end of the year came the role of Eleonora in Wolf-Ferrari's comic opera, taken from Goldoni's play, *The Inquisitive Women*, which deals with wives, who, suspecting that their husbands are having orgies at their club, smuggle themselves within its portals only to discover that the orgies are of a purely gastronomic nature. Neither was an opera in which Kiri has sung since, if indeed anyone has, and one rather wonders how useful it was to the students to take up time in preparing them.

After these two esoteric ventures, Kiri's first role of 1967 was an altogether more substantial one. Purcell's hour-long opera *Dido and Aeneas*, with a text by Nahum Tate, was first performed at Josias Priest's School for Girls in Chelsea in 1689, and has ever since been universally acknowledged as one of the supreme masterpieces of English opera. Lord Harewood, writing in the current edition of Kobbé's Complete Opera Book, refers to Purcell's 'uniquely beautiful ending to the opera', and describes Dido's closing scene, and aria 'When I am laid in earth' as 'one of the greatest moments in all opera'. Though listed in Purcell's original score as 'soprano', the role of Dido today is more usually taken by a mezzo-soprano. In recent years it has had Joan Cross, Kirsten Flagstad, Teresa Berganza and, perhaps most notably and memorably, Dame Janet Baker amongst its exponents. Perhaps it can be most accurately described as a role for low soprano, and certainly it suited Kiri's voice at that time admirably. She had begun to learn and rehearse the part straight after Christmas for a rather exciting public premiere on 15 March. Exciting because it was not to take place in the lugubriously cavernous auditorium of the Opera Centre, but across the channel at the Conservatoire of the ancient city of Caen in Normandy, where the performance was to be given as part of British Week.

In fact the Opera Centre provided Caen with another New Zealander, Paul Neal, as Aeneas, as well as Kiri's Dido, and the performance was rapturously received by the French audience, causing Kiri to repeat Dido's final, suicidal aria. This led to the headline in the local French paper: 'On Tuesday evening, for our pleasure, Dido killed herself twice,' and, even better, the paper's critic went on 'What can we say, however, of the beautiful, the royal Kiri Te Kanawa, of her exceptional voice, the mastery of which should lead her to the firmament of operatic stars?' Once again Kiri had proved her ability to respond to an audience.

As we have seen, when this performance was repeated three months later at the Purcell Room in London it was greeted with similar enthusiasm by the English critic Alan Blyth, writing in the *Daily Express* and, of more lasting significance, he amplified that praise, with a deeper analysis of Kiri's potential quality when he wrote in the August issue of *Opera*, the magazine which is the bible of opera-goers and performers alike. He noted: 'Her voice is warm, round, effortlessly produced and – apart from too much tone in the repeated "remember me" in "When I am laid in earth" – she used it with great intelligence in matters of phrasing and emotional weight. The reverberant Purcell Room accoustics *may* have flattered the quality of her voice, but I doubt it. In addition to her vocal attributes, her appearance was dignified and riveting – she needed no costumes to conjure up the Carthaginian Queen's plight.'

Kiri's next engagement at the Opera Centre, and her last before she flew out to New Zealand to marry Desmond, brought her back to earth with a bump as well as introducing her to a producer who has probably done more than any to develop and shape her subsequent career. John Copley, ten years older than Kiri, had studied with Joan Cross at the London Opera Centre's predecessor, the National School of Opera, and in 1950 he had appeared as the Apprentice in Benjamin Britten's *Peter Grimes* at Covent Garden. After completing his studies he had become a stage manager with Sadler's Wells Opera and, still in his early twenties, had successfully produced there Puccini's one-act opera *Il Tabarro* in 1957. He had moved from the Wells to Covent Garden as a staff producer and, by 1967, was a highly experienced operatic director with about a dozen productions and revivals to his credit. For the students at the Opera Centre to have John Copley as producer of a classic like Mozart's *The Magic Flute* was therefore a great advantage, as well as a searching and decisive challenge of their musical competence and stage sense.

For this production Kiri had been cast in the relatively minor mezzo role of the second of the Three Ladies who attend the Queen of the Night and who preside over Tamino and Papageno in the opera's opening scene. Three of her compatriots took leading roles: her old friend and rival Malvina Major was to sing Pamina, Kiri's Aeneas, Paul Neal, was Papageno, and another old friend from Auckland, Ann Gordon, sang the Queen of the Night. John Copley's first meeting with Kiri was far from being a case of love at first sight. In contrast to the other, more earnest students at the Centre he found her, 'Rather a silly girl then. I think at that stage she was very unhappy and didn't have many friends. She had been suddenly plummeted into what was, in retrospect, a pretty hideous set-up where there was a lot to criticize – and Kiri is a person who will always criticize. People there resented the fact that she could just get on a plane, do some concerts in New Zealand, and come back with £2,000. We were all rather poor then, and she'd come in with yet another new outfit. I don't think she ever meant it unkindly, but

Above: Kiri, aged about three, on holiday with Tom, her father, at·Puketuri.

Right: Ready to enter for the Gisborne Competition Society's dancing prize at the age of six.

Below: Kiri (*back row, third from left*) with Raewyn Blade (*fourth from left*) in a production of Romberg's *The Student Prince* in Auckland, 1962.

Above: Runner-up in the Mobil Song Quest at Hamilton in 1963, with winner Malvina Major and their teacher, Sister Mary Leo.

Right: Showing Sister Mary Leo the winner's medal after winning the Melbourne *Sun* aria competition in 1965.

Below: 1966: with Tom and Nell at a party in their garden at Blockhouse Bay, the day before Kiri's departure for London.

Above: An early role in 1966, as the Marquis de Bluette in Delibes' *Le Roi l'a dit* at the London Opera Centre.

Below: Mezzo to soprano: the crucial masterclass with Richard Bonynge at the London Opera Centre in 1966.

Above: 'Nothing like it since the Springbok Test!' Entering St Patrick's cathedral, Auckland, with a Maori guard of honour, August 1967.

Left: Now Mrs Park; with Desmond after the service.

Opposite:
Above: In the title role of Donizetti's *Anna Bolena* at the London Opera Centre's 1967 production.

Top Right: As Blanche de la Force in Poulenc's *Dialogues des Carmelites* in the London Opera Centre's summer production in 1968.

Right: As Carmen in the New Zealand opera company's production of Bizet's *Carmen* in 1969

Above: Two of Kiri's
early supporters:
Sir John Tooley,
general director of
the Royal Opera House,
Covent Garden;
and Sir Colin Davis,
music director of
the Royal Opera since
Kiri joined the company
in 1970.

Left: Mme Vera Rozsa,
Kiri's teacher, sternest
critic and strongest
supporter.

With HM Queen Elizabeth II and conductor, the late Walter Susskind, after singing at the royal concert in Dunedin town hall, 1970.

Getting ready, with Inia Te Wiata, to sing for New Zealand at Japan's Expo '70 in Osaka.

Kiri's first principal role at Covent Garden: as Xenia with Boris Christoff in the title role of Moussorgsky's *Boris Godunov*, 1971.

The step to stardom: singing the Countess in Covent Garden's new production of Mozart's *The Marriage of Figaro*, 1971.

Left: Jean Mallandaine, who coached Kiri through the new roles that followed her success in *The Marriage of Figaro*.

Below: At New Zealand House in London after a Waitangi Day concert, with Sir Bernard Fergusson, later Lord Ballantrae, a past Governor-General of New Zealand.

A Face for the Seventies: photographed by Lord Snowdon for
a *Sunday Times* magazine feature in 1972.

'I tried to make a bit of a fuss of her, to let her know she was among friends.'
Jon Vickers was Kiri's Otello when she made her New York Metropolitan
debut in Verdi's *Otello* as Desdemona at three hours' notice, in 1973.

Opposite:
Above: With Placido Domingo as Don José and Kiri as Micaela in Covent
Garden's new production of Bizet's *Carmen* in 1973.

Below: With HM Queen Elizabeth the Queen Mother in the Crush Bar at the
Royal Opera House following the gala premiere of this production. Also (*left to
right*) Sir Georg Solti, who conducted, Shirley Verrett, who sang Carmen, and
Sir John Tooley.

Kiri as Desdemona in Act I's love duet of Verdi's *Otello* in Covent Garden's revival in 1974. Her Otello is Carlo Cossutta.

Below left: Rehearsing the role of Marguerite with John Copley, the producer, and Stuart Burrows as Faust, for Covent Garden's new production of Gounod's *Faust* in 1974.

Below right: Marguerite's mad scene from the same production.

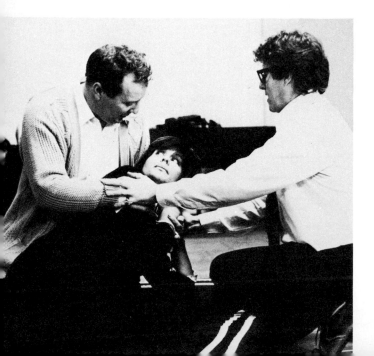

At a reception at the Paris Opéra with the then President of France, Valery Giscard d'Estaing and (*left to right*) Mme Giscard, Mme Pompidou and Grace Bumbry.

As Mimì in the last act of Puccini's *La Bohème* with Luciano Pavarotti as Rodolfo and (*left*) Thomas Allen as Marcello in Covent Garden's 1976 revival.

Above: Tatiana's letter
letter scene in
Tchaikovsky's *Eugene
Onegin* at Covent
Garden, 1976.

Right: With Desmond,
her manager Basil
Horsfield (*right*) and her
American agent Sam
Niefeld in the dressing-
room after the dress
rehearsal of the same
production.

people were aware of the fact that she was so much better off than they were.' His doubts about Kiri were not resolved by working with her in *The Magic Flute*. 'I remember sending her home because she hadn't learned her words. She was lazy and upset the rest of the cast. Quite honestly I wasn't impressed at all, and at that stage I didn't even find her beautiful. I think she's become a beauty now that she's grown up, though even then she was a beauty once she was on stage.'

When one considers that John Copley was responsible for Kiri's first great triumph, as the Countess in Covent Garden's new production of *The Marriage of Figaro* just four years later, and has subsequently directed her in very many important new productions and revivals both in Britain and abroad, one can appreciate the honesty and objectivity of these criticisms. Moreover, despite his misgivings, June Hall recognizes Copley's enormous help to Kiri from the outset. 'I think John really made it all happen. He was very, very patient, and when it came to the Countess, by which time I was working at Covent Garden myself, he had more patience than I could ever have given him credit for.'

Despite Copley's disenchantment with his Second Lady, the production of *The Magic Flute* went well and received a good measure of critical attention and approval. The *Daily Telegraph*'s critic, under the headline 'Magic Flute earns credit all round', wrote that 'Joan Carden, Kiri Te Kanawa, and Marjory McMichael blended charmingly as the Three Ladies, but I thought Miss Te Kanawa's warm, vibrant voice would probably have suited the part of the First Lady better.' The First Lady is of course a higher, soprano part. Malvina Major was singled out by the critic of *The Times* as 'an artist who should be watched', and *Opera*'s editor, the much respected Harold Rosenthal, writing in that magazine's September 1967 issue, while disliking Adrian Mitchell's new English translation, applauded Copley's simple, never dull, yet gimmick-free production, and found: 'The standard of singing was on the whole good, if not outstanding – one was impressed far more by the young singers' conceptions and musical style than their vocal abilities.' Copley's

[65]

original criticisms of Kiri's approach to her work, as she now freely admits, had been justified, however, and something needed to be done. Now that she and Desmond were happily settled together as man and wife in De Vere Gardens things looked distinctly more promising and there would henceforth be no excuse for any lack of application on her part.

When Kiri and Desmond arrived back in London in September 1967 they had moved straight into De Vere Gardens, thus being spared the time-consuming and expensive problem of finding a home. Veronica Haigh, though in New Zealand at the time, had been unable to attend their wedding but had seen them during their honeymoon and herself returned to London some months later, moving into the second floor and leaving Kiri and Desmond the run of the house. She recalls that once married, 'Kiri became exceedingly domesticated, bought a Cordon Bleu cookery course, and got down to things in a big way.' Cookery is indeed a talent that Kiri acquired then and has never lost: she remains a superb, creative cook who prefers to do things herself rather than have them done for her. A meal prepared at home by Kiri, however simple, is invariably a gastronomic experience. Miss Haigh also observed that Kiri was now working harder. 'She would practise much more at home. Once the next-door neighbour complained that there was singing going on, and I had to tell her that she was listening to a voice that she'd have to pay thousands to hear one of these days!'

Raewyn Blade, who had been unable to be one of Kiri's brides-maids because she was now performing in the musical *The Canterbury Tales* in London's West End, also continued initially to live with them at De Vere Gardens but she soon saw that, inevitably, their relationship had changed since Kiri's marriage, and that it would be better for both of them if she found somewhere else to live. 'I suppose I felt ousted as we'd been through so much together. I didn't want our friendship to suffer, so I moved to a flat in Gloucester Road. I met Michael Spring in May 1968 and we were married exactly a year later. Kiri and I have remained the best of friends,' and one of the loveliest things about her is that whenever she's been away abroad, she'll ring me up within twenty-four hours of getting back.'

For Kiri the process of building a marriage was a happy and fulfilling one. 'Des immediately started looking for a job. We were pretty broke, but I think those broke times were the best of our life. Des would give me some money on a Monday and I had to carry it through to the next Monday: it was marvellous – the first time I'd ever had to think of someone else. He found some freelance contract drafting work in engineering initially and then moved to a big mining finance company in the City of London early in 1968. As far as having children was concerned, at that stage I felt we weren't financially stable enough to have a family. I couldn't start having a family and then start having a job. If I was to do any good with my work, I should try now, before a family – it seemed more logical at that point to get on with my career.'

The next step in pursuit of her career involved the preparation for performance of four scenes in the title role of Donizetti's *Anna Bolena*. This opera about King Henry VIII's ill-fated second wife, Ann Boleyn, was written in 1830; it had been a great favourite with the *bel canto* prima donnas of the nineteenth century but had then fallen out of favour. Thanks to the great dramatic artistry of Maria Callas it had enjoyed a triumphant revival at La Scala, Milan in 1957, in a production by Luchino Visconti, and had been given in England at the Glyndebourne Festival, with the Turkish soprano Leyla Gencer in the title role, in 1965. The opera's closing scene, as the condemned Ann Boleyn awaits her execution in the Tower of London, leading to the aria 'Al dolce guidami' is a mad scene which Lord Harewood, writing in Kobbé, considers 'to vie with those from *Sonnambula*, *I Puritani* and *Lucia di Lammermoor* . . . It is one of Donizetti's great masterpieces of melodic and dramatic inspiration.'

The excerpts were presented at the Opera Centre in December, in a rudimentary staging by Tom Hawkes, together with scenes from Verdi's *Aida* and Humperdinck's *Hansel and Gretel*; and Kiri, with the young Australian soprano Joan Carden as Ann's rival and supplanter, Jane Seymour, appeared in only half of the performances,

[67]

sharing their roles with Donna Faye Carr and Teresa Cahill. She thus missed a notice from *Opera*'s critic, Arthur Jacobs, who saw the performance given by the other two ladies, but she did receive an appreciative review from Douglas Blake in *The Stage* who, under the headline 'Impressive singing at the London Opera Centre' wrote 'At the first performance the Anna was Kiri Te Kanawa, a young soprano of genuine promise, whose range of tone, colour and expression seems well suited to such parts.' Sadly, Kiri has not in fact sung any *bel canto* roles since, but those few performances were nevertheless to have one lasting and particularly beneficial effect upon her career.

Amongst those who went to hear *Anna Bolena* at the Opera Centre was a young artists' agent named Basil Horsfield. He himself had studied conducting and singing, as well as piano, violin and clarinet, at the Guildhall School of Music; he had set up as an agent just a few years earlier, initially managing only three artists: the conductor John Pritchard, the fine bass-baritone Geraint Evans, and the pianist John Ogdon. He had by 1967 added such distinguished singers as the American mezzo-soprano Shirley Verrett, and the tenors Stuart Burrows, George Shirley and Ryland Davies to his roster, and was constantly on the look-out for new talent and promising careers. Basil Horsfield still vividly remembers his first encounter with Kiri. 'I was struck by her entrance in the final scene – a long entrance without singing a note. I was convinced before she even opened her mouth that she had tremendous potential. It was her personality on stage that struck me even more than her voice – which was very good, though she wasn't using it properly. But theatrically she was way ahead of the others in personality and potential.'

After hearing Kiri in *Anna Bolena*, Horsfield contacted James Robertson who, as well as being the Opera Centre's Director, had conducted the performance. 'After that,' says Kiri, 'James called me into his office and said there was an agent interested who might like to represent me. I went a few days later, trembling and nervous, to Basil's office which was then up near the Angel, and found a great tall man towering over me. He said he didn't know what he could do for me at the moment, but asked if I'd like to be on his books.' Desmond recalls, 'Kiri felt very honoured that an agent wanted to take her on, and at first she stood in considerable awe of him. It was very much a case of "Mr Horsfield, sir".' It was in fact a crucial step in her career, for ever since Basil Horsfield and his partner John Davern – an Australian who had begun in the law and moved over to music – have developed, managed and encouraged every aspect of Kiri's work to her enormous advantage. More than that, they both rank now amongst her closest friends – godparents to her two children – not merely managers but part of a happy and united family. It is a fortunate singer indeed who has this kind of uninterrupted and unwavering support from the outset of her career, and it says a great deal for Basil Horsfield's musical intelligence and perception that he was able to spot Kiri's true potential so early on and, having had his hunch, played it so decisively.

Kiri completed 1967 by finding herself featured in the *Daily Mail*'s Charles Greville diary column – Nigel Dempster's less abrasive predecessor – three days after Christmas. Beside a large, and somewhat unflattering photograph of a girl with long dark hair and bushy eyebrows ran a headline: 'A dolly among the opera singers.' The diarist informed his readers that Kiri was 'not only pleasing to look at, but James Robertson, Director of the London Opera Centre where she is studying, says her voice is "the most beautiful we've heard for years". More modestly Miss Kanawa (*sic*) a twenty-three-year-old Maori says: "It's a great hulking voice".'

1968 was a year of further study and consolidation at the Opera Centre and of gradual, but tangible, movement towards a professional career as an opera singer in Britain. As an overseas student from the Commonwealth, Kiri still had to be granted official Home Office permission to remain in the United Kingdom from year to year. Accordingly John Kentish, the Opera Centre's Director of Studies, wrote to the Immigration Office in High Holborn in February 1968 to certify that 'Mrs Desmond Park (professionally known as Miss Kiri Te Kanawa) is a student at the London Opera Centre' and that 'It has been decided that in order to complete her

[69]

studies Miss Te Kanawa should remain at the London Opera Centre for a further twelve months.'

During her studies Kiri made a professional operatic appearance with Northern Opera in Newcastle-upon-Tyne, under the aegis of James Robertson, who was conducting Bizet's *Carmen* there and on a limited tour. The question of Kiri singing Carmen had already arisen during her visit to New Zealand for her marriage the previous August. An event during that visit had been the award of a 'Golden Disc' by the New Zealand Federation of Phonographic Industries for the sales of her long playing album *Kiri*, issued by Kiwi Records. This popular success had prompted the New Zealand Opera Company to offer her the role of Carmen Jones in performances of Oscar Hammerstein II's remarkably successful musical comedy. This used an all-black cast, and had up-dated Prosper Mérimée's setting of a cigarette factory in Seville to a wartime American parachute workshop, and turned the toreador Escamillo into a boxing champion. In the film the late Dorothy Dandridge was a memorable Carmen Jones, with the young Marilyn Horne singing the role on the soundtrack. Kiri eventually decided not to take the role, telling the New Zealand press that it might hurt her image. This drew an amusing rejoinder from Ojay Jones in the *New Zealand Evening Post*: 'In opera, especially, the particular girl must choose her parts carefully. The original Carmen, for instance, would be out: she was no plaster saint. *The Magic Flute*'s Queen of the Night is no social worker either. Musetta in *La Bohème* and Marguerite in *Faust* are both weak types. As for Don Giovanni's women – by the time he had finished with them, they had nothing left but their image, and that wasn't worth writing home about.'

Kiri, however, though she declined the Preminger version, agreed to Robertson's suggestion that she sing Bizet's original, both in Newcastle and again the following year, still with Robertson conducting, back in New Zealand. The Newcastle performances went well; they were a success both at the box-office and in terms of enthusiastic reviews in the local press. But Kiri was not entirely happy with the role. 'I enjoyed Carmen in some ways, but I got very bored with the music, and the character didn't really suit me.' Nevertheless, it was a paid professional engagement, though Desmond wryly recalls a performance given in Wrexham on the Welsh borders when, 'We drove up there in the Zephyr in filthy weather and the windscreen broke. We had to stay the night, get there and back and pay petrol and a hotel bill. By the time we'd done all that, we'd spent more than twice the fee!' James Robertson concedes now that Kiri 'is not a natural Carmen, and when I suggested she did it again she was very friendly but insisted that it wasn't right for her'.

Sally Sloman, however, recalls that the New Zealand performances were not entirely without incident, nor did they remain untouched by Kiri's schoolgirl sense of humour. 'I was watching from the wings, and at the dramatic moment in Act 3 when José aims his rifle into the wings and shoots, Kiri naughtily threw a stuffed duck out onto the stage. The well-known Australian tenor, Donald Smith, was not at all amused and took his revenge on her in the final "death" scene, with very "bruised" results!' Kiri has in fact returned to the opera since, but not in the role of Carmen. She took the part of Micaela, with Shirley Verrett as Carmen, Placido Domingo as Don José and Sir Georg Solti conducting, in Michael Geliot's new production at Covent Garden in June 1973, and subsequently recorded the role in a complete recording of the opera for Decca, again with Solti conducting. Although she now claims to have outgrown that role too, and would not care to sing it again, there is no question that the part of Micaela lies perfectly for her voice, and that the character of a simple, honest, above all loyal, country girl fits her altogether better than the volatile gypsy.

Another French opera, Poulenc's *Dialogue of the Carmelites*, had been chosen as the Opera Centre's major summer production. It had received its first performance at La Scala, Milan in 1957 and was produced at Covent Garden the following year, conducted by Rafael Kubelik, with Elsie Morison playing Sister Blanche and Joan Sutherland and Sylvia Fisher also in the cast. The opera concerns an incident during the French Revolution when a group of Carmelite

[71]

nuns from the convent at Compiègne were executed by guillotine in Paris. Emmet Lavery's libretto is a setting of an unused film scenario by Georges Bernanos, which had itself been inspired by a novel by the German author Gertrud von le Fort. The opera's principal character is Blanche de la Force, a young aristocrat who leaves her parental home for the Carmelite convent in order to find salvation. She later runs away from the convent to escape the threat of the Revolution and imminent martyrdom, but finally arrives at the scaffold just in time to follow her sisters in giving themselves up to the guillotine for God and their faith. Writing about the production in the *Financial Times*, the paper's critic, Andrew Porter, explained that the opera was concerned 'with inward states of mind, particularly the fear of death and its conquest by faith. The opera's main character, Blanche de la Force, is obsessed with fear. It drives her to seek refuge in the convent, where she is forced to witness the "bad death" of the old prioress who befriended and understood her. Fear drives her away again from the convent when the Terror threatens. Finally she is enabled to overcome it and join her sisters on the scaffold.'

It was thus a role which taxed not only Kiri's vocal training and resources – Blanche is on stage for much of the opera – but also her dramatic ability. Faced once more with the challenge of an audience – first in Bristol and then in London – but much helped by a careful and sympathetic producer, Tom Hawkes – she scored a resounding critical success (she shared the role with Teresa Cahill). In the article already referred to Andrew Porter wrote: 'The big role of Blanche was undertaken by the very promising Kiri Te Kanawa, who has a warm, lyrical voice with a timbre not unlike Marie Collier, and an expressive face which suggested poor Blanche's terror with a restrained dignity that was effective even on a stage necessarily almost always dimly lit.' The *Daily Telegraph*'s critic, Martin Cooper, also praised her performance, writing: 'Kiri Te Kanawa's full-bodied, yet well modulated voice made her a touching Blanche,' and Noel Goodwin in the *Daily Express* found that she was 'often vividly expressive'. Best of all, perhaps, was Stanley Sadie's notice in *The Times*: 'Blanche was sung by a New Zealander of rich promise, Kiri

[72]

Te Kanawa: a large, well-focussed soprano voice which she knows how (and when) to colour – her passionate, tremulous note of fear was very telling.' Dr Sadie also approved of Tom Hawkes's 'straightforward and effective' production and Reginald Woolley's 'strongly atmospheric' sets. His notice was surmounted by a large photograph of Kiri in her habit with Marjory McMichael, who sang the old Prioress. *The Carmelites* was sung in Joseph Machlis's English translation and James Robertson conducted the Bristol-based BBC Training Orchestra – hence the performances in that city. Another member of the cast who received good notices was Alexandra Gordon, Kiri's old friend from New Zealand, who played Sister Constance, Blanche's closest friend in the convent. Finally, her performance, as well as obtaining such approving reviews, also attracted her first 'feature' in a national newspaper. T. S. Ferguson included a substantial interview with Kiri in his Arts Diary in the *Sunday Telegraph* of 30 July together with her photograph – again in nun's habit. All told it had been a highly successful venture – though once again in a role she has never sung since.

Her final role of 1968 was again a professional engagement. This time it was with the Chelsea Opera Group, who give meticulously prepared concert performances of relatively little known operas and were then, as now, constantly on the look-out for promising young operatic voices. Again it was a role that she has not repeated: that of Idamantes, son of Idomeneo in Mozart's great *opera seria* about the Cretan King. When Mozart composed *Idomeneo* in 1780 – when he was only twenty-four – he wrote the part of Idamantes for the great male soprano Del Prato – to whom he referred as '*mio molto amato castrato del Prato*' – and it was del Prato who sang in the Munich premiere in January 1781. When the opera was given in Vienna five years later by a cast of well-born amateur singers, it included a tenor Idamantes, for whom Mozart had to transpose the music so as not to upset the part-writing. William Mann, writing in his comprehensive and stimulating book *The Operas of Mozart* (Cassell, 1977) tells us: 'In modern performances Idamantes is usually given to a tenor, occasionally to a female

[73]

soprano. Neither compromise is really satisfactory, either in the arias or the ensembles; we need the robust, brilliant colour of a male soprano voice or, in post-*coltello* days, of a male counter-tenor with a radiant masculine tone-colour and a strong upper register extending to top A.'

Colin Davis had conducted a concert performance of *Idomeneo* in the Festival Hall that May and had used there a tenor Idamantes, Ryland Davies (as he did when later recording the opera for Philips), but when the opera was produced at Covent Garden a decade later he had Dame Janet Baker singing the role. In October 1968 the critics, therefore, welcomed Chelsea Opera Group's decision to cast a soprano as Idamantes for their performance in the Queen Elizabeth Hall and, the following month, at Oxford and Cambridge. The performances were conducted by Roger Norrington – now Musical Director of Kent Opera and a stickler for authenticity in Mozart – and had Kenneth Bowen in the title role (Adrian de Peyer in Oxford), Marie Hayward as Elektra, and another Opera Centre student, Alison Hargan, as the Trojan princess Ilia, with whom Idamantes is in love.

Once again the performances went well and drew appreciative notices, not least for Kiri as Idamantes. In the *Financial Times* Andrew Porter wrote: 'Splendid to hear a soprano Idamantes. Even in the theatre I would prefer one; at a concert performance (or in a recording) the case for a soprano hardly needs to be argued. The Group had found a girl with a fresh, frank, clear tone, Kiri Te Kanawa, from the Opera Centre, who in "Non ho colpa" sounded more like a youthful, impetuous prince than any tenor, dropping his line an octave down to be submerged in the accompaniment, could hope to do.' In *Opera* of December 1968 that early discoverer of Kiri's talents, Alan Blyth, wrote: 'In both aria and ensemble the advantage of Idamantes being a soprano was self-evident, and Kiri Te Kanawa, that most promising New Zealand soprano, who was appropriately attired in a trouser-suit, had just the right clear, pungent tone for the role. At present she is a rather impassive performer; but a good producer – and more attention on her part to

[74]

consonants – could put that to rights.'

In the face of such warmly voiced praise, it seems the greater pity that Kiri has never sung the role since. But perhaps there is still time. Though Vera Rozsa (Kiri's present teacher) feels that if she were to sing in *Idomeneo* again, she would be better suited to the role of Ilia, the Trojan princess, whose character has enormous potential and whose music, she believes, would suit Kiri's voice admirably. At any event *Idomeneo* made a fitting climax to a year of consolidation and substantial progress, and meant that Kiri could look forward to 1969, the year she was due to finish at the Opera Centre, with some degree of optimism.

7

Vera Rozsa and Covent Garden

FROM THE BEGINNING OF 1969 until the end of 1970 was a crucial period in Kiri's life. During those two years she left the London Opera Centre and thus ceased to be a student; she found the singing teacher who has watched over her ever since; she was offered a contract as a junior principal by the Royal Opera House; and she moved with Desmond to a new home in Surrey. The first major event of 1969, however, was her glossiest professional engagement to date.

During February at the Royal Festival Hall, as part of the London Philharmonic Orchestra's season, there was a concert performance of Handel's opera *Alcina* with Joan Sutherland in the title role (one she had sung in a new production at Covent Garden seven years earlier and had subsequently recorded for Decca). The orchestra was conducted, as usual in Sutherland performances, by her husband Richard Bonynge, and the distinguished cast included Margreta Elkins, Monica Sinclair and Ryland Davies. Partly as a result of Bonynge having previously heard her at the Opera Centre, Kiri was offered the small *travesti* role of the young nobleman Oberto who spends much of the opera searching for his father – who has in fact been turned into a lion by the sorceress Alcina. Quite aside from the glamour of being able to stand beside the great Joan Sutherland on the platform of a packed Festival Hall, this concert also offered the opportunity to regale the audience with two fine Handelian arias, and Kiri's performance went well. Another exciting project early in

1969 involved a trip to Monte Carlo, where Decca were recording Giordano's opera *Fedora* with Magda Olivero in the title role, and the famous tenor Mario del Monaco and great baritone Tito Gobbi in the leading male roles. Once again Kiri's was a small, 'trouser' role – Dimitri, a groom – but again it offered her the invaluable experience of working alongside the operatic first division.

It was, however, in another of those lesser known operas that Kiri made her biggest impact during 1969. Since its foundation in 1954, originally as the St Pancras Arts Festival, the Camden Festival had made a speciality of unearthing rare or forgotten operas, and during the 1960s these were performed in the old St Pancras Town Hall – now the Library – in Euston Road, opposite St Pancras Station. It was far from an ideal auditorium, having neither pit for the orchestra nor raked seats for the audience; but year after year devotees of neglected operas would flock to St Pancras to sit and listen amongst the potted palms. (It's fair to say that although the small, modern Collegiate Theatre in Gordon Street round the corner, which has now replaced the old Town Hall as Camden's operatic venue, is splendidly equipped and has superior acoustics, the atmosphere there has never seemed the same.)

For the 1969 Festival Camden's choice had fallen upon Rossini's *La donna del Lago*, taken by his librettist Tottola from a French translation of Sir Walter Scott's six-canto poem 'The Lady of the Lake'. The opera was first performed at the San Carlo opera house in Naples in 1819, with the great soprano Isabella Colbran singing Ellen, 'The Lady'. It came to London in 1823 and was highly successful up to the middle of the nineteenth century. Thereafter it suffered a decline and from 1860 doesn't appear to have been performed again until a revival under Tullio Serafin at the Maggio Musicale in Florence in 1958, when Rossini's original finale 'tanti affetti in tal momento' was omitted. Nevertheless, writing in Kobbé, Lord Harewood considers: 'It is full of graceful, expressive music and amounts to one of Rossini's most attractively lyrical scores. That it suffered a century of neglect may perhaps be attributed to three factors: the role of Ellen was written for Colbran and is lyrical

[77]

until the taxingly brilliant final aria, which puts it out of consideration for most sopranos or mezzos; the two tenor roles bristle with high notes, cascade with runs and roulades, and yet demand to be sung with a consistent smoothness out of each of most singers for the past hundred years or so; and – most important – the story is concerned with characters of a much lower voltage than the Normas, Lucias, or early Verdi heroines who supplanted them in the imagination of a later generation.'

It was the role of Ellen, with original final aria restored, that Kiri took in May 1969. Her three lovers: Hubert (in fact James V of Scotland in disguise), Roderick and Malcolm were sung by the tenors Maurice Arthur and John Serge, with the young British mezzo-soprano Gillian Knight in the *travesti* role of Malcolm. Once again Tom Hawkes was the producer and the opera was conducted by Gerald Gover. Writing an extended 'profile' of Kiri in *Opera* of July 1981, the highly experienced critic, Elizabeth Forbes, vividly remembered the occasion: 'On an evening in May 1969, London opera lovers flocked to Camden Town Hall to hear one of the rarities typical of the Camden Festival, *La donna del lago*, Rossini's operatic version of the poem by Sir Walter Scott, "The Lady of the Lake". The curtain rose on the first scene, representing the banks of Loch Katrine at dawn. Morning mist hung heavily over the loch – the smoke machine had been too generously used – and after the opening chorus of Huntsmen had gone off in search of prey, a ravishing female voice was heard from an invisible boat on the loch, where Ellen, the Lady of the Lake, waited for the return of her lover. At last the mist dispersed and a girl, whose appearance matched the beauty of her voice, became visible, seated in her boat. For many people in the audience, myself included, that was the first glimpse of Kiri Te Kanawa, the Maori soprano, then twenty-five years old.'

There were a clutch of enthusiastic reviews for her performance, with the *Daily Express* headlining its notice 'Maori is best of Italian Scots', and going on to say: 'She not only looks the kind of girl to set the clans at loggerheads, but she also has a warmly expressive voice with a good grasp of Rossini's special vocal style.' Writing in

Opera of July 1969 Alan Blyth observed that her 'warm, fresh tone, easily produced, gave much pleasure especially in "Tanti affetti". Her stage presence is too placid, her acting too rudimentary, so that she conveyed little of Ellen's predicament.' Here Alan Blyth had put his finger on Kiri's most significant weakness then: a lack of dramatic conviction, which stemmed fundamentally from an insufficiently deep knowledge of the music. In those days Kiri would mostly absorb parts by learning the music by heart, relying on her excellent ear, retentive memory and instinctive musical sense, rather than fully comprehending them through studying the score and really getting to know the music. Basil Horsfield was not slow to appreciate that and was determined to find a singing teacher who would really make Kiri work and thus bring out the best in her. Meanwhile Kiri went off to New Zealand to repeat her Carmen performances under James Robertson on tour out there, which were received with habitual enthusiasm by the New Zealand press and audiences.

When she returned to London in the autumn of 1969 Kiri had to face the challenge of becoming a full-time professional singer. Fortunately for the moment money was not a major problem: Desmond was well established in his consultancy job with a London-based international mining company and was spending an increasing amount of time on site abroad, particularly in the Middle East, which meant that all his expenses were found for up to half of the year. They were still living, for very little rent, in Veronica Haigh's house in De Vere Gardens but they were both coming to the conclusion that it was time they found a home of their own. Miss Haigh was due back in London to spend a year in her house and, however good their relationship, the prospect of living as a married couple in somebody else's home and having to fit in, was not ideal. However, if they were going to buy a home it would mean that Kiri must have a regular income too.

Upon her return, therefore, Kiri began to audition, first for Sadler's Wells – now the English National – Opera at the London Coliseum who, curiously, never contacted her after the audition at all. Next, Basil Horsfield suggested, she should try the Royal Opera

House, Covent Garden. So began a frustrating period: Kiri believes she auditioned for the Royal Opera no fewer than nine times. Even if that is slight retrospective exaggeration it is certain that a substantial number of auditions took place. One of the problems, Kiri feels today, was that her reputation for laziness and indiscipline had preceded her from the Opera Centre. Thus, although Joan Ingpen, then the Royal Opera's Controller of Planning (which meant casting) and John Tooley, assistant to and about to succeed the retiring General Administrator, Sir David Webster, had both heard her sing at the Opera Centre and were highly enthusiastic at audition about her potential, the Musical Director, Sir Georg Solti, and some of his music staff were at that stage rather less so. 'They could see I was lazy and could hear I sang flat – mainly because my poor old voice was still changing: it was like a young man whose voice is breaking and there's suddenly a terrible squeak in the middle!' Unluckily she also contracted mild hepatitis and had to sing another audition for Solti when 'I was on all sorts of glucose, just trying to get some energy from somewhere.'

Two people who heard her and were impressed were Colin Davis and Peter Hall. Although in the end the grand plan never materialized, at that stage these two were scheduled to take over as joint directors at Covent Garden of music and staging, at the beginning of the 1971–2 season following the retirement of Sir Georg Solti from the Musical Directorship in July 1971. The first new production of their joint directorship was to be Mozart's *The Marriage of Figaro*, conducted by Davis and produced by Hall. Although it was the kind of prestigious new production for which Covent Garden could have chosen and been accepted by most of the world's leading singers, for some reason that Davis no longer remembers – but possibly connected with the fact that Hall planned to give *Figaro* the first time round in English and then in Italian on its first revival – the role of the Countess had not yet been cast.

Colin Davis heard Kiri first. 'Jimmy Gibson had told me this girl was singing at the Opera Centre. She came for an audition and I think she sang 'Salce' from Verdi's *Otello* and something else which

I don't remember. I couldn't believe it, so I said, 'Let's hear her again,' and so we did, just to make sure we hadn't been under some magic spell! I hadn't heard such a beautiful voice for years and years and years. Then Peter came and heard her too.' Peter Hall recalls: 'We were both bowled over but we asked her to come and do it again a fortnight later: it happens very rarely that there is no possibility of doubt. I cannot think of many times that it's happened in my life. I remember, for example, when I was Director of the Royal Shakespeare Company, David Warner walked on for his audition, did a speech from Richard II and I said, "There's my next Hamlet." It was like that with Kiri – clearly a remarkable talent and we could see the potential. I'm not a professional musician, though I'm musical and I know about singing. As some actors speak lines and I don't hear what they say, a lot of singers sing very adroitly and it means nothing. What I found immediately impelling about Kiri was that it meant something to me: when she opened her voice, it meant. And she is blessed with what I would think is one of the most beautiful voices in the world.'

John Tooley was likewise impressed. 'I was David Webster's assistant at that time. I heard both the auditions she gave for Colin and Peter, and of course I'd heard her before at the Opera Centre. It was a very, very remarkable voice, the freshness and openness both in the kind of sound she was making and in her as a personality. I remember thinking here was something very special: you just had to sit up when Kiri sang, because here was an undoubted talent that was likely to go a long way.'

Eventually Kiri was offered a three-year contract as a junior principal at the Royal Opera House from the beginning of the 1970–1 season, at a starting wage of £50 per week, which was negotiable after one year. 'It seemed a fortune then, and Des and I thought we were on Cloud Nine: he was earning good money with his expenses paid a lot of the time, and now we had a joint income.' From the artistic as well as the financial point of view, the stability of becoming a member of the Royal Opera company was of unquestionable advantage to her. John Tooley, who became General Administrator at the same time as Kiri joined the company, now says: 'She needed it. Kiri needed to have her life well planned, with time to learn new roles in a sensible manner. We also wanted to be sure that we would be able to lay out a progressive plan for her.'

The other major professional development at the end of 1969 was Kiri's change of singing teacher. For some time her lessons with Florence Norberg had not been achieving as much as either teacher or pupil would have liked. Their personal relations were as good as ever, but the vital musical and interpretative progress was not being made. Miss Norberg had already mentioned another teacher to Kiri who might be able to take her on. This was Vera Rozsa, a Hungarian who had studied singing in Budapest, and who had sung regularly at the Vienna State Opera as a mezzo-soprano during the early 1950s before moving on to Rome, and then marrying and coming to live in England in 1953. Initially she gave many song recitals, then went to the Royal Northern College of Music in Manchester and met the great teacher Frederic Cox, who suggested that she began teaching some students there. By 1969 Madame Rozsa was living in London and beginning to establish a very considerable reputation as a singing teacher. Among her pupils was the highly promising mezzo-soprano, Anne Howells, then married to Ryland Davies, the Welsh tenor managed by Basil Horsfield. Anne Howells had met Kiri from time to time at the Opera Centre and had suggested to Basil Horsfield that Vera Rozsa might be the right kind of teacher for Kiri. Anne contacted Madame Rozsa and asked her if she would consider taking Kiri on: she had heard Kiri sing at the Opera Centre and had been impressed by her voice, and was thus certainly not averse to taking her as a pupil. But before anything she telephoned Florence Norberg, who told her that if anyone else was to take Kiri on, she would be very happy if it were Vera. So Kiri came for her first meeting and lesson with the lady who has most closely supervised and directed her singing and professional career ever since and whom she freely acknowledges to be the bedrock of her success.

Vera Rozsa remembers the early meetings well. 'She was very sweet when she came to me, but at our second or third lesson she tried to find out what kind of teacher I was. She said she had to go for a long holiday to New Zealand and asked what I thought. I replied she had to make up her own mind and that nobody could do that for her. She gave up the holiday. I summed up Kiri from the beginning as a tremendously independent person. From the beginning, therefore, we got on very well, and she has never played me up (though we've had a few crises) and she's never been late for a lesson.' Madame Rozsa was immediately impressed by Kiri's voice. 'From the beginning it was an outstanding and beautiful voice, and the quality was magnificent. When she came to me she had already tackled the upper middle range, and she was a natural soprano. I don't think that her early training had been bad, but her voice is naturally light, and I think some of her teachers had tried to make it much bigger.'

For Kiri another great advantage of being taught by Vera Rozsa was the latter's practical operatic experience, as a result of which she does not teach on a merely technical basis. Madame Rozsa explains: 'Some teachers are marvellous but teach only voice production. I won't separate that from the music itself, so that I teach interpretation and everything else together.' It was this wholeness of approach and emphasis on interpretation that were to enable Kiri to make the fullest use of her natural and instinctive assets and thus to prepare completely rounded performances and would lead to her enormous success at Covent Garden as the Countess in *The Marriage of Figaro* at the end of 1971. Without the intervention of Vera Rozsa and the fact that Kiri responded so positively both to her teaching and to her splendidly volatile and intelligent personality, it is doubtful whether she would have been ready to achieve that kind of success in a major role.

By the beginning of 1970 Kiri and Desmond had found a house they felt they could be happy in. It was near Esher, in Surrey, about fourteen miles from the centre of London, on a private estate in what, in the fifteenth century, had been the grounds of Esher Palace. Cardinal Wolsey had moved there from Hampton Court when he fell from King Henry VIII's graces; by 1970 all that was left of the

[83]

palace was a small building called Wolsey's Tower, standing at one corner of the estate. Neither Kiri nor Desmond can now remember how they decided upon Esher, but Kiri knew she wanted a house with some land around it. 'We'd looked at apartments in town and I'd decided there was no way I'd live in one of those grotty little flats, which were so expensive anyway. I can't think of anything worse than coming home to the third floor and a pot plant on the window-sill. This was a three-bedroomed house with a rather abysmal reception area – but it had an enormous field of about fifty acres right next door, with cows in it, and you could see squirrels and rabbits on the lawn.'

Fortunately for Kiri, who up to then had done no more than sing the tiny role of one of the bridesmaids in Mozart's *The Marriage of Figaro* in a concert performance under the great veteran conductor Otto Klemperer at the Festival Hall, an offer now came up which would materially help to pay for the house. This was for a ten-concert tour of New Zealand, accompanied by her old friend and mentor, Barbara Connelly. It involved performances in places such as the Bay of Plenty, Napier, Hawke's Bay and Waihato as well as Wellington and Auckland, and in some cases in open-air auditoria to audiences of several thousands. In her programmes she included such popular songs as 'Show me', 'Love, this is my song', 'As long as he needs me', 'Climb every mountain' and 'Edelweiss', as well as her current London repertoire of operatic arias and songs by Dvorak and Rachmaninov. Needless to say the performances ended with the virtually obligatory Maori medley, culminating in the unaccompanied 'Pokare Kare' as her farewell to the audience. Equally needless to say, there followed a massive adulatory coverage in the New Zealand press, and in addition to the fees from the concerts another album of popular hits for Kiwi Records provided welcome additional income.

For Kiri the real pleasure in this particular visit to New Zealand stemmed from the fact that it coincided with a state visit to the country by the Queen, the Duke of Edinburgh, Prince Charles and Princess Anne. On Wednesday, 18 March she was invited to sing at Dunedin Town Hall with the NZBC Symphony Orchestra conducted by Walter Susskind at a royal concert. Here she performed in the first half Leonora's aria 'Pace, pace mio dio' from *La Forza del Destino* and 'Doretta's dream' from Puccini's *La Rondine* – her latest complete opera recording to date, made in 1981 – and, in the second half, after the arrival of the royal party, Carmen's 'Habanera' and, backed by the two hundred and seventy-strong Combined Dunedin Choir, her eternally popular Nuns' Chorus from *Casanova*. It was a momentous day – as well as singing for the Queen and being presented to her afterwards, Kiri had earlier been one of some twenty prominent New Zealanders (including a cabinet minister, a supreme court judge, church leaders, prominent academics, and the leader of Dunedin and Otago's Maori community) who were invited to luncheon on board the royal yacht *Britannia* in Dunedin Harbour.

The meal, accompanied by a musical selection played by the band of the Royal Marines, was a marvellous occasion which Kiri remembers vividly. 'I was still being auditioned by Covent Garden at the time I'd left England, and when I was introduced to the Queen she said to one of her aides, "I think she should be at Covent Garden, don't you?" So when I went to my final audition in London and was offered a contract, I felt totally convinced that the Queen had rung up Covent Garden and told them to have me at the Royal Opera!' This occasion in Dunedin was the first at which Kiri met Prince Charles whom she found, along with his sister Princess Anne, 'Adorable – utterly charming people.'

Having completed the concert tour in March, Kiri returned to England and she and Desmond moved house to Esher. She auditioned again for Covent Garden, was finally accepted, caught up on some lessons with Vera Rozsa, and then in June 1970 was back in New Zealand again, preparing for an exciting trip on her country's behalf to Osaka in Japan. New Zealand had a pavilion at the World Exhibition called Expo'70, and on New Zealand's National Day, 8 July, attended by the Prime Minister Keith Holyoake, an all-day performance entitled 'Kiwi in The Sun' was presented. As well as Kiri, New Zealand's other Maori opera singer, the fine bass Inia Te

Wiata, sang there; tragically he died of cancer the following year. Inia, already well established in England and singing regularly at Covent Garden, had been a great friend to Kiri when she had first arrived in London as a student, had visited her and Raewyn several times at their flat in Forest Hill, and had ever since kept something of a fatherly eye on his fellow Maori. By 1970 Te Wiata had seen his young friend realize her vocal potential and was able to tell the New Zealand *Weekly News*' correspondent: 'She stands out on the stage: she's such a natural mover, and she's got that marvellous personality.' The Kiwi show went extremely well; Kiri scored a great hit with the Japanese audience by adding four Japanese folk-songs, sung in their language, to her performances of Maori songs and a special version of the national song, 'God defend New Zealand'. It was immensely satisfying to be an ambassador for her country at the age of twenty-six. One result of her visits to her homeland was that she was chosen as New Zealand's 'Entertainer of the Year' in September, but by then she was hard at work back in London, and the trophy was accepted on her behalf by Tom, her father, and was passed on to her mother who was in an Auckland hospital recovering from an operation.

1970 was the year of Beethoven's bicentenary, and in London this involved Kiri in the performance of a major 'discovery' of the bicentenary year, the composer's early cantata on the death of the Emperor Joseph II, written by Beethoven when he was nineteen but not in fact performed until sixty years after his death, and only rarely since. A performance was given at the Royal Festival Hall by the BBC Symphony Orchestra, Chorus and Choral Society under Colin Davis who, having heard Kiri audition for Covent Garden and been much impressed, had chosen Kiri as the soprano soloist, a part which he felt lay very well for her. The music in parts looks forward to Beethoven's opera *Fidelio*, and it is the soprano soloist who has most to do. Kiri didn't duck her opportunity and was rewarded by favourable notices in the national press, of which perhaps the happiest was Noel Goodwin's in the *Daily Express* which, under the headline 'Maori girl triumphs', said: 'Superb singing last night by Kiri Te Kanawa suggested that Covent Garden has acquired a

[86]

valuable investment for the future in putting this young Maori soprano under contract. Her performances since she came to Britain four years ago have shown her as a singer with a future – and the future is now, the present . . . The soprano gets a major share of the solos, and Miss Te Kanawa phrased them with a musician's feeling as well as vocal beauty.'

Two days later Kiri went down to Plymouth to give a recital in the city's central hall as part of New Zealand Week. She was accompanied by the young New Zealand conductor, John Matheson, who was also about to join the staff at Covent Garden – to become one of her most helpful coaches during her early years there. The Plymouth audience were given 'Oh quante volte' from Bellini's opera *I Capuleti e i Montecchi* (based on Shakespeare's *Romeo and Juliet*), the 'Seguidilla from *Carmen*, 'Dove sono' from *The Marriage of Figaro* (which she was already preparing for Covent Garden), Dvorak's Gypsy Songs, two numbers from Gershwin's *Porgy and Bess*, 'Vilja' from *The Merry Widow* and finally, a group of Maori songs. The critic of the local *Western Evening Herald* found her a delightful soprano, with style, zest and beautiful control, but observed: 'Her voice is not yet sufficiently developed to reach the heights of grand opera as, despite her ample middle register, she was uncertain in her top notes in the operatic section.' Her other major engagement of late 1970 was at the Royal Albert Hall with the Royal Choral Society, conducted by Meredith Davies, taking the soprano solos in Honegger's comparatively rarely heard biblical oratorio *King David*, with the distinguished actor Richard Attenborough as narrator. But, as the year drew to a close, perhaps the most pleasing thing was to see her photograph in the *Daily Mail* of 24 November, standing on the main staircase of the Royal Opera House along with five other new 'recruits' – Delia Wallis, Teresa Cahill, Norma Burrowes, Alison Hargan, and Nan Christie – over the headline 'Just to show that opera singers aren't all overweight and over thirty', and a caption which pointed out that all six young sopranos were due to make their debuts during the coming year. It certainly made an attractive picture and augured well for the future.

[87]

8

The Marriage of Figaro

THE YEAR 1971 was totally different. It was Kiri's first working year
on contract to Covent Garden; this meant a succession of roles
during the course of the season leading up to her appearance in
December as the Countess in Mozart's *The Marriage of Figaro*, the
Royal Opera's first new production of the following season. She had
a 'dry-run' as the Countess at Santa Fe in the United States during the
summer as well as concerts at regular intervals and recordings for
Colin Davis of some of Mozart's church music, and for Sir Georg
Solti of Wagner's *Parsifal* in Vienna.

Although her first year at Covent Garden had an unquestionably
happy outcome, it meant far harder work and a far more disciplined
approach than Kiri had ever previously experienced. She says now,
'For that first year I felt as if I were totally occupied with Covent
Garden. I may have done other things but, apart from Santa Fe, I
can't really remember them now. I'd already learned *Figaro* in
English, as that had been Covent Garden's and Peter Hall's original
plan, and I sang it in English in Santa Fe. But by then I'd had to
learn it in Italian as well, for which Ubaldo Gardini, the Garden's
wonderful Italian coach, was responsible. Then there was Jimmy
Gibson, the Head of Music Staff, regularly checking up on my
progress; and Geoffrey Tate, one of the repetiteurs, from whom I
caught hepatitis (though it's a standing joke between us now), was

[88]

teaching me the role of the Countess. Colin Davis would see me from time to time and ask how it was going – he was also getting weekly reports on me from Geoffrey. Effectively, Covent Garden were paying for me to have a formal education.' Of course, in addition to this intensive period of study at the Royal Opera House, she was also going at least once a week to North-West London for lessons with Vera Rozsa who was also working with her on *Figaro* – interpretation of the role as well as the music.

Kiri's first job at Covent Garden in 1971 was to 'cover' – understudy – the role of the slavegirl Liu in Puccini's *Turandot*, with Birgit Nilsson in the title role. She already knew Liu's two arias, having performed them at early concerts back in New Zealand, but in fact neither of the sopranos taking the role had to drop out of any performances, so Kiri's portrayal of Liu was never seen on stage. The *Turandot* performances, however, filled January and February; March and early April were spent working with Colin Davis on his set of recordings of Mozart's Church music. These involved, so far as Kiri was concerned, the *Vesperae solennes de confessore*, K.339, the *Kyrie in D minor*, K.341, the late *Ave verum corpus*, K.618, and the ever popular *Exsultate jubilate*, K.165, which she has frequently performed at concerts ever since. The boxed set of four records, using a large number of soloists, was issued by Philips in 1972; it was reviewed in the authoritative *Gramophone* magazine by their experienced critic Trevor Harvey. His analysis of Kiri's achievement at that stage is interesting, particularly if one bears in mind that she recorded this music some six months before singing in *Figaro* at Covent Garden. 'On this evidence,' he wrote, 'she seems to be rather variable in quality. At the start I thought her good, but nothing special. Yet she sings 'Laudate dominum' very beautifully. In *Exsultate jubilate* her words are poorish, but in coloratura passages her voice flows so easily that I could readily forgive her anything. I don't find her line elsewhere consistently beautiful, yet she does the end of the central slow music of this piece very movingly, while her coloratura in the well-known "Alleluia" finale is sheer joy.' Far from being damnation with faint phrase, this was the sort of assessment of which any debutante had every right to feel proud.

Next in April came her Covent Garden debut, in the unlikely role – in the light of her subsequent career – of the leading Flower Maiden in Wagner's *Parsifal*. The first night was on 21 April, and public attention was focussed primarily on two things that evening. Firstly, that Covent Garden's staff conductor Reginald Goodall, having been neglected by the Royal Opera for over a decade, was making his come-back after establishing his name as one of the great Wagnerian conductors of the day by his performances of *The Mastersingers* and the *Ring* Cycle at the Coliseum with Sadler's Wells Opera. Secondly, that on this first night the scheduled Gurnemanz, Franz Crass, was ill, and the magnificent Wagnerian bass Gottlob Frick, now aged sixty-five, had emerged from retirement in Vienna to sing the role. The evening lasted from six until eleven-thirty and interval discussion was inevitably about Goodall's slow tempi and Frick's resplendent performance, so one might have forgiven the critics for neglecting the Flower Maidens in their notices. Not a bit of it: in *The Guardian* the late Philip Hope-Wallace wrote: 'The bevy of floral vamps was led by a soprano with a really glorious voice and presence: Kirite Ke Kanawa (*sic*) is her New Zealand name.' And in the *Sunday Times* another eminent critic, Desmond Shawe-Taylor, commented: 'The six flower maidens (all admirable, led by the pure and perfectly focussed high sopranos of Kiri Te Kanawa and Alison Hargan) had evidently been rehearsed with exceptional thoroughness.' In *Music and Musicians* John Greenhalgh noted that the Flower Maidens 'were led by the admirable, outstanding Kiri Te Kanawa', and in *Opera* Alan Blyth observed of the group that 'Instead of the usual wobbling Wagnerian sopranos and mezzos, we heard some of our most promising, fresh-voiced young ladies, among whom Kiri Te Kanawa and Alison Hargan were outstanding'. For Kiri these favourable notices were some consolation for an uneasy rehearsal period with Goodall, whom she remembers 'looking at me in disdain, as much as to say, what's she doing here? None of us had "names" and he was very disappointed. The only person he knew was Anne Howells, who was already famous; with the rest of us he clearly thought he'd been given some bum steers!'

No sooner was the last night of *Parsifal*'s run completed on 12 May, than Kiri opened on the 13th with a role in another massive opera. As the Tsar's daughter Xenia in Moussorgsky's *Boris Godunov* she was presented with another problem, that of singing in Russian, even if phonetically. The reason for this was the presence in the title role of the formidable Bulgarian bass, Boris Christoff, who insisted on singing the opera in its mother tongue so that an otherwise entirely English-speaking cast had to follow suit. The sad thing about *Boris Godunov* was that it should have provided Kiri with her first chance to be on stage at Covent Garden with her friend and fellow-Maori, Inia Te Wiata. He had been cast, as in the previous season's revival, in the role of the monk, Pimen. In March 1971 the *New Zealand Herald* had carried a report from its London correspondent pointing out that they had never sung together in Britain before, and quoting Te Wiata as saying: 'Kiri's voice was considered right for Boris's daughter, and I'm delighted that two Maoris will be singing at Covent Garden at the same time. It's never happened before.' Nor did it happen, for in June Inia Te Wiata died, tragically young, of cancer, leaving behind him not only a widow and a young child but also an exquisitely beautiful but alas unfinished traditional Maori carving. This may be admired as his memorial in New Zealand House in the Haymarket.

However, as a consolation, Kiri found it interesting to be working with the great Christoff, who was in the habit of talking to young sopranos in his dressing-room during performances. She recalls being summoned there one night, and then shortly afterwards being summoned on stage by the internal tannoy! Christoff would not let her leave and she had to be 'rescued' by the stage manager. The performances went well and Kiri looked quite stunning in her blonde wig, singing her one solo aria exquisitely and collecting her usual clutch of enthusiastic notices. In *The Times* the paper's arts editor, John Higgins, wrote: 'Christoff found himself with a new Xenia, Kiri Te Kanawa, who is due to sing the Countess in next season's new *Figaro*. It is an attractive voice, full and easy flowing; the stage manner is immensely attractive, and on the evidence of last night's brief appearance Miss Te Kanawa can act. She deserves watching closely.' This performance also drew her first notice – again an approving one – from *Opera*'s distinguished and encyclopaedically knowledgeable editor, Harold Rosenthal, who noted her 'attractive and full-toned Xenia'.

At the beginning of July Kiri left England for the United States to make her operatic debut there at the Santa Fe Festival in New Mexico, which had been founded by its General Director, John Crosby, in 1957. The opera house is beautifully set amidst rocky, mountainous desert countryside, having a covered stage while the audience sits in the open air. For *Figaro* this meant that the stage's back wall could be removed for the final 'garden' act so that it could be played against a 'backcloth' of moon and stars in a summer's night sky, as Mozart had written it. Basil Horsfield had originally planned this American series as a 'dry-run' for the English-language production she would be performing in December at Covent Garden. But now that she was learning it in Italian for the Garden, she had also to re-learn it in the English translation of Americans Ruth and Thomas Martin for Santa Fe, which she found laborious. Moreover, rehearsals did not go entirely smoothly, especially when the producer, Bliss Herbert, insisted that the Count should smack his wife's face in Act 2. Kiri protested that this was contrary to the characters of the Count and Countess but was overruled. She concedes now that Jean-Pierre Ponnelle had precisely the same idea when directing her in the role for television in 1976, and that at that more experienced point in her career she was happy to comply.

Another untoward incident that Desmond remembers well was the time Kiri was bitten by a possibly rabid Siamese cat. He was working in Atlanta, Georgia at the time she was in Santa Fe; Kiri used to phone him every night for a long chat, and one evening told him she had been bitten by a rabid Siamese cat. Of course it had to be proved rabid before she could have the necessary and unpleasant injections. So the State Police went looking for it – and fortunately found it, discovering that it wasn't rabid after all. A more cheerful episode occurred at Lloyd's restaurant in Albuquerque, where the chef, Fred Johnson, had created a new dish of shrimps, fresh pineapple and water chestnuts. Lloyd's head waiter, Jody Romero, decided to name this somewhat unlikely combination 'Shrimp Te Kanawa' after Kiri, explaining, 'She's exotic, and so is the dish.'

Figaro opened at the end of July, and in the cast with Kiri was another highly promising young singer, also on the threshold of an international career. This was the American mezzo-soprano, Frederica von Stade, who was singing the role of the page, Cherubino (she would repeat it with Kiri again as Countess at the Glyndebourne Festival in Peter Hall's superb production two years later). Kiri and 'Flicka' took to each other at once and have been the greatest of friends ever since. The performances went well and were warmly received by the local press, who variously referred to Kiri as 'stunning and impressive' and 'the highlight of the evening'. Quite aside from that sort of praise, she also had the more tangible advantage of a visit to the production by the agent Sam Niefeld of Columbia Artists, who had gone there at Basil Horsfield's suggestion and who 'arrived in a large car to take me out, and swept me off my feet'. He signed up Kiri for American representation there and then, so that after her Covent Garden Countess had aroused enormous interest in America, other agents of a less enterprising disposition discovered that she had already been snapped up that summer by Sam Niefeld – at Santa Fe. Another distinguished visitor to those performances was the veteran General Director of the San Francisco Opera, the Viennese Kurt Herbert Adler, who was to remain in charge there until the autumn of 1981. He was so impressed by both Kiri and Frederica von Stade that he promptly engaged both of them to appear in San Francisco's production of *The Marriage of Figaro* in September of the following year, thus beginning for Kiri a happy and virtually continuous relationship with one of her favourite opera houses and best-loved cities.

Almost as soon as Kiri got back to England from Santa Fe she began to prepare the Countess again, this time with John Copley.

'The point was that, of all people concerned, it was John who absolutely didn't want me to do the part – he wanted me out most of all. He'd seen me at the Opera Centre and knew I was a lazy, useless woman, and he didn't think I was old enough or experienced enough. I didn't resent him for it because I knew he had his reputation at stake – it was his big chance too. But I looked on it as my opportunity to take the bull by the horns and I thought, "I'm going to hang on there". I had to prove myself, and I did, and John's initial opposition urged me on. I liked him very much even then, and now he's a great friend. But at the time he insisted on my beginning to work on *Figaro* six weeks before "the stars" got there because he said I had to be as good as "the stars" when they arrived. I worked my guts out to be as good as them. It worked, because in the first few weeks of working together John could see I was being serious. He could see I was going to sing it well, and that I was trying my damnedest to act it. I did everything he said and I loved it: for me the rehearsals went too quickly.' Copley himself doesn't disagree with any of this and says now: 'Working on *Figaro* she couldn't have been more concentrated and brilliant. She was amazing in it, and worked really very hard. The only other time she's worked as hard as that with me was when we did *La Traviata* together in Australia at the Sydney Opera House, another great success for her.' At the time Kiri acknowledged John Copley's contribution to Duff Hart-Davis of the *Sunday Telegraph*, who was writing an extended feature article on the production and its rehearsals. 'He's changed me completely. I used to be a bit of a tomboy, but he taught me to walk and sit properly. He made me into a *lady*! His attention to detail is fantastic – he even made me start growing my fingernails long.'

Once the whole cast did come together to rehearse the production Kiri found, with one exception, that she got on splendidly with them. The cast consisted of Geraint Evans as Figaro; the Canadian baritone Victor Braun as the Count; Patricia Kern taking Cherubino; two fellow New Zealanders – though she did not know them – Heather Begg and Noel Mangin, as Marcellina and Bartolo; first John Lanigan then Alexander Oliver when Lanigan took ill as Don

Basilio; another young soprano, Lillian Watson, singing Barbarina; and the German-based American soprano, Reri Grist, as Susanna. She remembers, 'Geraint was adorable to me – a honey – I couldn't have had a nicer colleague and, despite his great experience and his reputation for sometimes telling young singers what to do, he absolutely never tried to advise me or anything like that – he never doubted me for a minute. Heather Begg was adorable too, and so was Victor Braun. The only problem I had was with Reri Grist, who resented me. I did have a fracas with her on stage once during rehearsals, and I remember another day her coming up to me and saying, "What you are doing is elementary", and I replied that I knew that but I just wanted to do my job. She was a bit hard on me, but I thought, "That's the way the stars come in and she's just trying to show me she's a star." I tried to follow my mother's advice never to let the sun go down on an argument, and to make sure that even if we couldn't be friends, we'd be friendly acquaintances. I hoped then that I wouldn't be like that when I got to her age! I wanted to be a little kinder to the younger singers and speak to the under-studies and try to help them.' So she did. I myself went to most of the rehearsals of Covent Garden's revival of *La Traviata*, in which Kiri was singing Violetta for the first time in London, at the London Opera Centre in December 1979. A very young and promising soprano, Claire Powell, was making her Royal Opera debut as Violetta's maid Annina. It was heart-warming to watch Claire Powell's diffidence and uncertainty melt away in the face of Kiri's kindness and warmth, and above all her professional interest, as the rehearsals progressed.

As the rehearsals for Figaro continued it became apparent to Colin Davis, John Copley and to the cast, that the production was developing remarkably well and that Kiri's Countess was going to be something special. She herself remembers sitting with Victor Braun in the Nag's Head, the pub opposite Covent Garden's stage door, shortly before the first night, when he said to her: 'You know, Kiri, you're going to have a really terrific success.' She replied, 'Oh don't talk stupid – I'm only a student. I'll make my way through it

[95]

and do my best – but as to having a great success, much as I'd like it, I don't think it's possible.'

But Victor Braun was right. I was at *The Marriage of Figaro*'s first night on Wednesday, 1 December 1971, and from the moment the house lights went down and the overture set off at Colin Davis's exhilarating pace, we could feel that something special was in the air, even more so when the curtain rose on Stefanos Lazaridis's beautiful, lived-in, sun-baked Spanish country house and we saw Reri Grist's Susanna looking exquisitely pretty in Michael Stennett's costume, while Geraint Evans's inimitable Figaro, on hands and knees, measured their prospective bedroom. The first act went splendidly, but of course the Countess doesn't appear in it. Desmond had spent that act in the bar rather than the auditorium, consuming quantities of gin and tonic to give himself strength for his wife's first appearance at the start of Act 2. He could have saved his money. The curtain rose again on a very young and very beautiful woman in an elegant flowing dress with a wide, low, lace-trimmed neckline, and lacey cuffs on sleeves which finished at the elbows, a poised, if sad, expression and wonderfully glowing, burnished copper skin. When, a few moments later, she opened her mouth and began to sing 'Porgi amor' (Love, grant me some solace for my pain) – surely the most cruelly testing entrance for a soprano in any opera, offering no chance for the voice to warm up, no dialogue, no recitative, nothing but the first words of the aria after a very short orchestral introduction – it was apparent that here was a quite remarkable talent.

The applause after the aria was considerable, and the atmosphere till the next curtain was electric as Kiri, moving with dignity and assurance, acting with considerable insight and expressiveness, and singing superbly, realized to a rare degree the wronged young wife of an unfaithful, yet jealous and overbearing husband. The mood in the crush bar during the interval that followed Act 2 was exultant. Here was a marvellous new production of everybody's favourite opera, immaculately conducted by the new Music Director, beauti-fully designed, magnificently sung, and with a new star – best of all a star discovered by Covent Garden itself – born before the audience's eyes.

Yet there was better still to come. In Act 3 comes the Countess's great recitative and aria 'E Susanne non vien . . . Dove sono i bei momenti di dolcezza e did piacer?' (Where are the lovely moments of sweetness and pleasure?) opening sadly, even wistfully, but ending on a proudly defiant note in both words and music: 'Ah! se la mia constanza nel languire amando ognor, mi portasse una speranza di cangiar l'ingrato cor' (Ah, if only my constancy which makes me love him even while I languish, can bring me the hope of turning his ungrateful heart!). At the end of the aria came her hurried, impulsive exit, stage right – and an ovation on a scale that is seldom heard from first night audiences of new productions at the Royal Opera House who faintly deprecate over-overt displays of enthusiasm. At that point, and with that applause, many a soprano would have returned on stage to take a bow, but Kiri did not do so – John Copley had coached her on that point too. 'After the dress rehearsal, which went very well, John came to me very seriously and said, "Now Kiri, there's one thing I want you to promise me. In the whole of your life, in my production and in anybody else's, you must promise me never to take a curtain call after 'Dove sono'. Not ever in your life." I said, "Yes John, I promise," and I've broken that promise only once, in Germany, and that time I was physically pushed on stage, which made me extremely angry. Now I always make straight for my dressing room and take off some piece of my costume so they can't get me back.' The interval talk in the crush bar following Act 3 was even more excitedly jubilant than before, and we returned eagerly for the final act, set in the garden. It was not perhaps as beautiful as Lazaridis's other settings, but was made totally enchanting by Kiri's appearance in the finale as she came on, dressed as Susanna, to sing her forgiveness of her errant husband. It was a moment of supreme emotion and rarely have I felt an opera house so genuinely moved.

Kiri says now, 'From the point of view of satisfaction, I thought I had satisfied myself – I had proved myself to me. I don't really know what the rest of the cast thought, but they all congratulated me afterwards. Des, of course, was over the top. I don't think I really thought about the reviews, because I'd proved it to myself, but I was dumbfounded by them – they were far in excess of what I deserved at that time. They'd found the new singer and went whoomph!'

That was certainly a fair description of the press reaction to her performance. The following morning all the papers hailed the production and with it, a new star. In *The Times* the paper's chief music critic, William Mann, an expert Mozartian, wrote: 'Fortunately in this production the Countess looks and moves like a teenage goddess; and though it is the most prominent role Kiri Te Kanawa has played at Covent Garden, she sings the two difficult arias and the equally important ensembles and recitatives with real dignity and assurance, and boldly spacious phrasing.' The *Daily Telegraph*'s critic, Robert Henderson, commented on 'a most impressive performance', and in Thursday's *Financial Times* the paper's much respected critic, Andrew Porter, contented himself with a large photograph of Kiri and Geraint Evans above a caption referring to 'A dignified memorable young Countess who sang . . . with a warmth of tone and an eloquent full-voiced line seldom heard in the role' and promised his readers a more detailed assessment the following day. When that appeared there was another large photograph of Kiri alone and a lengthy notice which concluded: 'Let us hasten to celebrate this youthful enchanting *Figaro*. Colin Davis's new regime could not have made a better start.' And about Kiri's performance: 'The new star is Kiri Te Kanawa. For years we have been praising this young New Zealand soprano . . . yet the promise of her performances had hardly prepared us for . . . well, frankly for such a Countess Almaviva as I have never heard before, not at Covent Garden, nor in Salzburg or Vienna, at once young, full-throated, a singer of great accomplishment and a vivid character . . . As an actress Miss Te Kanawa is accomplished. She commands the stage, wears costumes well. She was a young, beautiful, dignified, warm-hearted and affecting Countess.' Against this Philip Hope-

[98]

Wallace, the *Guardian's* veteran critic, whose memory extended back over nearly half a century of operatic performances, was more reserved in his appraisal, noting that she 'sang the music with attention. But the personality, the maturity of the character were absent, or only faintly discernible. She is too fresh an artist yet for this magical portrait of a wife experiencing first disillusion.' It was an assessment with which Kiri would today, in retrospect, be inclined to agree.

Yet Hope-Wallace's was increasingly a lone voice as Sunday's papers joined the chorus of acclaim. Desmond Shawe-Taylor – whose experience was as extended as Philip Hope-Wallace's – wrote in the *Sunday Times* that Kiri's Countess 'created a justifiable sensation . . . She has come far indeed: I should say to the threshold of international fame,' and, having praised her singing but observed 'I think she will come to make more use of her words,' he concluded: 'Since she has also a lovely stage presence, the enthusiasm of the house knew no bounds.' His colleague Peter Heyworth in the *Observer* declared that she merited a paragraph to herself and concluded it by saying: 'It was evident that we were in the presence of a singer of quite exceptional promise. Miss Te Kanawa not only has the emotional antennae of an artist, but the vocal resources and technique to give them flesh. The radiant tenderness with which this Rosina finally forgave her erring spouse was evidence enough that Covent Garden here has a pearl of great price.'

So it continued in the overseas press as well, with a report, photograph and interview by Anthony Lewis in the *New York Times* two weeks later, another in *Newsweek* at the beginning of January, and a reference in *Time* to 'pearly-voiced soprano Kiri Te Kanawa, who scored a sensation as the Countess'. Anxiety, however, was expressed by J. W. Lambert of the *Sunday Times*, who observed in the *Christian Science Monitor* that her performance 'made it clear that here was a future singer of world class' but concluded: 'Heaven preserve this young singer from over-exposure'. This caution was reiterated by *Opera*'s editor, Harold Rosenthal, who in the magazine's January issue devoted a lengthy leading article to his enthusiasm for the new production, though regretting that the original plan to perform it in English had been jettisoned. About Kiri he had this to say: 'Kiri Te Kanawa's Countess is, to be sure, not yet the very deep study it will obviously become – but she already has so much – youth, beauty and a voice of rich creamy quality, used exquisitely. She must not, indeed Covent Garden must not let this great talent be seduced away by offers of this or that role, for this or that large fee in the international circuit. We have seen this kind of thing happen before, it would be criminal if it happened in this case.'

So responsible, however, was Covent Garden's and Basil Horsfield's management of Kiri's career that Harold Rosenthal need not have worried. During 1972 she sang the Countess again at Covent Garden and also in San Francisco, and added just one role, Desdemona in Verdi's *Otello*, to her repertoire, singing that for Scottish Opera in Glasgow and Edinburgh. Despite a modest salary, regardless of what roles and how often she sang, Kiri was perfectly happy at that stage to remain under the wing of the Royal Opera House, and says now: 'I'd tasted a little success early on in New Zealand, and I knew about press coverage and all those things that follow a lot of exposure. Covent Garden offered me a five-year contract on the strength of *Figaro*. Basil rang me up and asked me if I wanted to do it, and Des asked me too. I said, "Well it keeps me here in England for a start, and I can still do little jobs outside and go away sometimes. I'm still learning my craft, and what better place to learn it than at Covent Garden?" Also, by staying in London I had Vera to pull me down to earth.'

After the first night of *Figaro* this return to earth had not been accomplished without a certain degree of pain. Kiri decided not to go to Vera for a lesson before the second performance, which was to be broadcast, the following week. Vera recalls: 'The second performance was the following Tuesday, and she didn't come for a lesson. I wondered whether I should call her or not, but I didn't, and the second performance wasn't so good. I listened to it on the radio, but I didn't say anything. But when Kiri asked me what I thought, I said, "It wasn't as good as the first, maybe you were tired or something." She was very angry and said that she never wanted to see me again, but the next day she forgave me – and came for a lesson!' John Copley had a similar experience. 'The second night of *Figaro* she sang like a drain because she was so nervous and couldn't believe her success. The third night she was back on form a bit, but not much. I went round to her dressing-room and said that it was a bit better, and she replied that it was marvellous. I told her it certainly wasn't and that she'd got to get it back. Then she did another five performances, and they *were* all marvellous.' Kiri entirely accepts the criticism now, and has never since sat back and done nothing after a successful first night. It was a case of a twenty-seven-year-old learning by experience, and Kiri was always prepared to learn.

The *Figaro* performances continued virtually until Christmas 1971, and between the fifth and sixth of them she made a rapid three-day trip to Vienna to record the Flower Maiden scenes of *Parsifal* for Decca, with Georg Solti conducting the Vienna Philharmonic Orchestra in the Sofiensaal. After a peaceful Christmas and New Year, spent taking a well-earned rest at home, her first engagement of 1972 – apart from an appearance on one of Geraint Evans's musical programmes for Harlech Television in Wales – was in Lyon in France for a series of five performances as the Countess in *Figaro*, beginning on 8 February. There was however one important new undertaking just before that Lyon *Figaro* opened. At the beginning of February she sang, for the first time, Richard Strauss's magnificent and moving *Four Last Songs* with the BBC Symphony Orchestra, conducted by John Pritchard. It was a formidable undertaking for a soprano still in her twenties and at the outset of her career, but Kiri loved the music and had worked extremely hard at it with Vera Rozsa who felt then, as she still does, that the songs lay absolutely perfectly for her voice. As Kiri puts it, 'I plunged right in at the deep end. I had to make a start on them, and you don't find out about something big until you've made mistakes.' The *Four Last Songs* have remained firmly in her repertory, and constantly performed ever since; in 1978 she recorded them for CBS Records with the London Symphony Orchestra conducted by the very promising young Andrew Davis, with impressive results.

In the *Figaro* cast in Lyon there was only one singer whom Kiri knew, Anne Howells who was singing Cherubino and with whom Kiri had become increasingly friendly since she joined the company at Covent Garden; they had moreover both been on the Vienna *Parsifal* trip in December. They shared a hotel room in Lyon and as Anne Howells recalls, 'We both hated it: it was supposed to be the best hotel in Lyon, but it was very expensive and Kiri was on some sort of economy drive. So one morning at 7.15, when I was still sound asleep, Kiri phoned my room and said, "Annie – it's Kiri here: can you hear that drilling noise outside?" I replied that I couldn't before as I'd been asleep but that I could now; and Kiri said, "Right – we're moving out to that cheap hotel where the others are staying!" So there and then we left, but not before Kiri had had a very mediterranean row with the hotel manager in the hall about the noise. The new place was very cheapskate with a horrible smelly lift. It was like entering a prison, and there was even more noise there because our rooms were right next to the kitchen!'

But it was just as well that Kiri was staying with a friend, because on the night of the last performance there was tragedy for her. Kiri remembers, 'We got back to the hotel and they told me there had been a phone call from New Zealand, which I thought very strange. We'd been intending to go out and eat, but I decided to stay in the hotel while Annie went to get pizzas. I was in the glass phone booth in the hall when she got back, taking the second call. It was my uncle Bill – I knew there must be something very wrong and asked what had happened. He said he'd got some very bad news and I asked quickly which one was it, praying it wouldn't be Daddy. I couldn't have stood it to be my father – somehow my mother was different. She was ten years older than him and she'd always prepared me for her death, telling me for years what to do "when I die". I knew she wasn't well, didn't look after herself and was over-weight, and that the doctors had warned her about heart attacks, but I still didn't really believe it could happen. The saddest thing of all was that the two of them were due to come to England to be with us for a year – it was the preparations for that that must have killed her. I remembered a few weeks earlier, back in London, I'd come home from rehearsing the *Four Last Songs* with John Pritchard one night when she rang me. I was tired and exhausted, and she said I hadn't written. I had, but the letters had been held up by the Christmas mail. I said, "Mummy, there must be at least six letters coming in," and all she could say was, "Darling, you never write." That was the last time I ever spoke to her. She never even heard me sing in an opera house, but at least she got to hear about the big splash I made in *Figaro* at Covent Garden before she died.'

Fortunately for Kiri not only was Anne Howells there to keep her company – but also, as she had just sung her last performance, there was nothing to stop her flying straight off to New Zealand. By a fortunate chance Desmond was already in Australia and able to join her there. Kiri returned to London, where Basil had sorted things out so that she could leave for Auckland immediately; she recalls that on the long flight, 'I didn't cry very much, or really let go, because there was so much to cope with, and I knew my father would be completely wiped out by it.' Once in New Zealand, the funeral took place, and then Tom Te Kanawa flew back to England with his daughter and son-in-law. By the time of Nell's death he had retired from his business, and he straight away got rid of the house in Block-house Bay, keeping just the cottage on Lake Taupo that he had built after the war as a holiday house and for his fishing. This remains his home in New Zealand today – the place where he lives if he is not with Kiri, Desmond and the grandchildren in England.

One happier event for Kiri, just before her mother's sudden death, had been to find herself in February in the *Sunday Times Magazine*'s collection of 'Faces for the Seventies'. Better still was the fact that her face, along with those of actresses Fiona Fullerton, Kika Markham, Sandy Ratcliff and the ballet dancer Diana Vere, had been photographed by Lord Snowdon. She found him friendly, informal, and highly professional to work with and particularly enjoyed the pub lunch they had together before 'shooting' started.

The result remains one of the most striking pictures to have been taken of her, and also one of the most truthful. Her face, virtually without make-up, is framed by the soft brown waves of her hair, she has a gentle, yet confident half-smile, and the portrait focusses on her superb, immense brown eyes. Kiri was already in France when the *Sunday Times* of 6 February appeared and astounded the newsvendor in Lyon by buying three copies instantly. 'He must have thought I was mad – British papers are so expensive in France!'

Once back in Esher with Desmond and her father, there was a series of off-stage priestesses to be sung in Covent Garden's revival of *Aida* during March and early April, plus a Good Friday performance of Handel's *Messiah* at the Royal Albert Hall with the Royal Choral Society and Royal Philharmonic Orchestra conducted by Meredith Davies. Then, in the middle of April, she left for Scotland to make her debut with Scottish Opera in her next major role, that of Othello's ill-fated young wife Desdemona in Verdi's magnificent *Otello*. Although Anthony Besch's production for Scottish Opera had first been seen in 1963 and had been revived many times since, there was nevertheless a full rehearsal period, which was to Kiri's advantage. The first night was not until 5 May in Glasgow's King's Theatre – Scottish Opera's base there until the splendidly renovated Theatre Royal became their new headquarters a few years later. Kiri found it a difficult time, for not only was this a new and complex, though relatively short, role, but she was also still suffering from the shock of her mother's death, which was now, finally, beginning to hit her.

She recalls that one day during rehearsals, 'I broke down and had to go home to the flat in the White House where I was staying. But Charles Craig (who was my Otello) and his wife were also there and were wonderful to me. They gave me something to eat and all was well.' Fortunately Kiri got on extremely well with Scottish Opera's General Administrator, Peter Hemmings, and with both her co-principals, Charles Craig and Peter Glossop, who was singing Iago. 'From Charles Craig I learned how to treat people, how to be nice to them. He'd been singing for years, knew the part backwards and I was just a raw beginner. Yet I had nothing but kindness from him and I never heard one nasty word from him about anybody. Peter Glossop was wonderful too. This big rough person with a strong northern accent, and yet with an utterly beautiful sound coming out every time he opened his mouth to sing. People had told me he was terrible to work with, but he wasn't at all. In fact I think I even tipped tomato ketchup all over his head one night!'

Scottish Opera's fine artistic and musical director, Alexander Gibson, was not conducting *Otello* that season. Instead the conductor was the well-known, highly experienced, but somewhat pedestrian Italian, Alberto Erede, from whom Kiri derived very little musical help. Admittedly she had her previous knowledge of the two last act set-pieces – the 'Willow Song' and the 'Ave Maria' – to fall back on, plus invaluable lessons with Vera, but this was not the same as being rehearsed by a really caring conductor of the Colin Davis or Alexander Gibson variety, and in the circumstances it is hardly surprising that her performance was both musically and dramatically incomplete. Basil Horsfield had arranged for Kiri to sing the role in Scotland so that she could learn the ropes before tackling it at the New York Met and then Covent Garden. However, her first attempt at Desdemona was received enthusiastically by the critics. The most perceptive notice came from Noel Goodwin, writing in the July issue of *Opera* who, having observed that, 'The conductor seemed more concerned to achieve force of dramatic impact than depth or range of expression,' and having commented favourably on the performances of Craig and Glossop, continued: 'Their experience might have intimidated a singer of less confidence and talent than Kiri Te Kanawa, who was singing her first Desdemona and who did so with a rare beauty of vocal tone and phrasing, if as yet lacking variety of expressive feeling. She needs only to become more familiar with the music and the character to become outstanding in the role, and to raise Desdemona's innocence from pathos into tragedy: the "Willow Song" and final scene were already very affecting.'

One great source of pleasure for Kiri that came from the Glasgow performance of *Otello* was that not only did Desmond come to see it but he brought Tom Te Kanawa with him to see his daughter on stage in an operatic role for the first time. Tom remembers being deeply moved by the performance, and by seeing his daughter looking quite different on the stage, a frail young woman in a blonde wig, totally removed from the healthy outdoor girl he had watched grow up in New Zealand. He also recalls his sadness that his wife Nell was not with him, as she should have been, to see Kiri's performance. He said afterwards to his daughter, 'If only mother could have been here with me – she would have loved to have seen you, and she never had the chance.' Kiri's reply was touchingly and comfortingly simple: 'But Daddy, she can see me now.' To sit beside Tom Te Kanawa, as I have done, when his daughter is performing in the opera house is in itself a moving experience. The fine-featured, extremely dignified, elderly Maori sits there with his eyes fixed on the stage, a broad smile of satisfaction on his face, and the tears coursing down his cheeks. Sadly however, as well as the joy of seeing his daughter on stage in *Otello*, there was also personal misfortune during Tom Te Kanawa's visit to Scotland. A keen golfer, it had always been one of his life's ambitions to play on the world-famous course at St Andrew's. This trip provided the perfect opportunity and a round was arranged with the Canadian bass Joseph Rouleau, another golfing enthusiast, who was singing Lodovico in *Otello* with Kiri. But on the first green poor Tom suddenly collapsed and had to be rushed to hospital for what turned out to be a prostatectomy. He has not tempted fate at St Andrew's a second time so his ambition remains unfulfilled.

Having sung seven performances of Desdemona in Glasgow, Aberdeen and Edinburgh during May and early June, Kiri headed south again to cover the role in Covent Garden's revival. Jon Vickers, who would sing it with her at her New York Metropolitan debut nearly two years later, was in the title tole; Joan Carlyle was singing Desdemona at the Garden and Kiri was not in fact required. Her next active engagement was at the Holland Festival in The Hague where she sang some Mozart arias, including 'Porgi amor' and 'Dove sono', accompanied by the Netherlands Chamber Orchestra conducted by David Zinman. Once again she was acclaimed by the press, and by audiences – this time in Dutch.

July was spent back in New Zealand under the auspices of the New Zealand Broadcasting Corporation. Kiri was contracted to undertake a tour which combined concerts with the NZBC Symphony Orchestra conducted by John Matheson and the Symphonia of Auckland under Juan Matteucci, with a series of recitals accompanied by her old friend, Barbara Connelly, at the piano. It was a packed itinerary, involving five concerts and six recitals between 8 and 31 July. Eleven performances in three weeks is not a schedule designed to improve the voice, and is the kind of thing Kiri has always tried to avoid. It is fair to say, however, that in July 1981 she took on something very similar, indeed even harder, when she sang seven performances of Donna Elvira in *Don Giovanni*, and four of Fiordiligi in *Così fan tutte* during the Royal Opera's Mozart Festival at Covent Garden between 6 and 24 July, and rounded off that marathon by singing an aria by Handel in St Paul's Cathedral five days later. On both occasions she was left feeling totally exhausted and vowing that she would never repeat the experience.

Another parallel between July 1972 and July 1981 was that in the earlier year, with Barbara Connelly, she had opened each of her New Zealand programmes with two Handel arias, the second of which was 'Let the bright seraphim' from *Samson*. Thus, nine years before the world watched her sing it on television, the aria was heard by audiences in Napier, New Plymouth, Auckland, Wellington, Hamilton and, perhaps best of all on 19 July, by a full house in the Regent Theatre, Gisborne, the town where Kiri had been born and had spent her childhood. For the orchestral concerts there were two programmes: one involved operatic arias, including 'Dove sono' and 'Ach, ich fühls', Pamina's aria from *The Magic Flute*, as well as Marguerite's 'Jewel Song' from Gounod's *Faust*; the other introduced a new role, that of the other Marguerite in Berlioz's strangely hybrid work *The Damnation of Faust*, which the composer planned as an opera, yet which tends to work better in concert performance.

Despite her heavy schedule, and being troubled initially by a heavy cold, Kiri, as always in her native land, sang to full and enormously enthusiastic houses, and drew fulsome notices from the local press wherever she sang, though they did rather grumble that Berlioz's Marguerite was an insufficiently dramatic and exciting role for their heroine, whilst applauding her assurance and vocal beauty in Strauss's *Four Last Songs* which she had included in all her recital programmes with Barbara. Nevertheless, after the final recital in Napier on 31 July, Kiri was extremely glad to fly back to London, en route to three weeks of well-earned rest with Desmond in Malta.

Next, in September, came performances of *The Marriage of Figaro* again, this time in San Francisco as part of the San Francisco Opera's Fiftieth Season. Amongst the cast she had friends in Geraint Evans, who was Figaro, and Frederica von Stade who was singing Cherubino, as she had done in Santa Fe. The young American soprano, Judith Blegen, sang Susanna, and the Count was the Swedish baritone Ingvar Wixell who has since sung in a variety of operas with Kiri in various opera houses and has become a much-liked colleague. He sang Scarpia to her first Tosca in Paris in March 1982. The revival of *Figaro* had five performances and drew thoroughly approving notices from the West Coast press before Kiri left San Francisco, a town which she had come to like enormously, for London again and to yet another series of *Figaro* performances at Covent Garden in October.

Possibly by then she was tired – she certainly had every reason to be – or was exhausting her sense of discovery of the role of the Countess. Possibly British music critics displayed that tendency to reconsider their verdict after they have given a unanimous and enthusiastic greeting to a new star. At any rate, at this Covent Garden revival the young Rumanian soprano, Ileana Cotrubas, was acclaimed, quite justifiably, for her performance as Susanna while, though still warm, the notices were rather more critical of Kiri's performance. In *The Times* William Mann expressed the view that, 'She needs to watch her pitch and quality of sound,' and Ronald Crichton in the *Financial Times* noted that her 'intonation wavered' in 'Porgi amor'. In the December issue of *Opera* Arthur Jacobs, having noted that 'Dove sono' won her a great ovation, continued: 'I am frankly puzzled. This young New Zealander has an appealing personality and a warm tone, but hers was a less than fully accomplished performance. The consonants were sometimes voiced too soon at the end of a syllable, the upper and lower reaches of the voice were not in full adjustment, and no decent trill was maintained at the end.' There were elements of accuracy in these observations, if somewhat churlishly expressed, but their effect was to make Kiri resolve thenceforth to have little to do with reviews. Nor does she, seldom troubling to read them and leaving Desmond to fill in time in front of the television during evenings at home by cutting out and filing the various notices of her performances. There is little point in complimenting Kiri on a superb review in such and such a paper: the odds are that she won't have read it. For Kiri the audience and its reaction has always come first, and she has preferred to leave the critics to their own, more rarified, devices.

9

The Beginning of Stardom

HAVING SEEN OUT 1972 with yet another series of *Figaro* performances in December, this time at the Grand Théâtre in Bordeaux, Kiri could look forward during 1973 to an extremely busy and stimulating year in which she would perform three new major roles for the first time. They were Micaela in *Carmen*, Amelia in Verdi's *Simone Boccanegra* and, perhaps most importantly for her, Donna Elvira in Mozart's *Don Giovanni*. In order to get to grips with learning them Covent Garden had awarded her the Drogheda-Mayer Fellowship for a month's study leave during January which she spent in Mantua, in Italy, with the distinguished singing teacher and coach, Maestro Campogalliani.

The year began with two prestigious engagements in a series of entertainments entitled 'Fanfare for Europe', a sort of festival which had been devised, largely by the then Prime Minister Edward Heath, to celebrate the entry of the United Kingdom into the European Economic Community. As a good New Zealander there was, of course, a certain piquancy in Kiri's participation, though she was but one of many distinguished Commonwealth artists who took part. The first of these engagements was on 3 January at the Royal Opera House when a Gala Performance of 'Fanfare for Europe' took place in the presence of the Queen and the Duke of Edinburgh. The entertainment was a celebration in words and music, devised by Patrick Garland and John Copley, designed to depict Britain's progress towards Europe. A galaxy of stars, of both the straight and lyric stage, participated, including Laurence Olivier, Tito Gobbi, Janet Baker, Elisabeth Schwarzkopf, Peter Pears, Sybil Thorndike, Max Adrian, Judi Dench, and Régine Crespin. Kiri's contribution was limited to one short item in the programme: the beautiful trio from the first act of Mozart's *Così fan tutte*, in which the two sisters, Fiordiligi and Dorabella, assisted by Don Alfonso, sadly wish their boyfriends a pleasant journey after their abrupt departure for the wars. Kiri was not in fact to sing the complete role of Fiordiligi in the opera house until 1976, but sang the trio on this occasion with Yvonne Minton and Richard Van Allan. Along with the other performers she was invited to a very grand supper party afterwards at Lancaster House. Their host was the Prime Minister who afterwards wrote, thanking her:

'Dear Kiri Te Kanawa, I wanted to write this line of thanks and congratulations to you for your contribution to the Gala Performance at Covent Garden on 3 January. It was a marvellous evening, worthy of the occasion it celebrated; and it was a special pleasure to see how naturally the British contribution (in which I include the Commonwealth contribution) dovetailed into the European contribution. In expressing my gratitude to you, I know that I write for all those present. With very best wishes. Yours sincerely, Edward Heath.'

Kiri's other contribution to the European fanfare was a performance at the Theatre Royal, Drury Lane of Marguerite in Berlioz's *The Damnation of Faust*, which she had sung the previous year during her New Zealand tour. This time John Pritchard was the conductor, with the New Philharmonia Orchestra and Huddersfield Choral Society and the Welsh tenor Stuart Burrows (who would become an increasingly close colleague and friend) as her Faust. Kiri's singing drew a clutch of highly enthusiastic notices, with the *Guardian*'s Philip Hope-Wallace, now fully won round to her quality, writing: 'As for the Marguerite, Kiri Te Kanawa won all hearts: graceful, heartfelt phrasing, and a tone of such crystalline purity as one hears once in a month of Sundays: a memorable contribution.' In the *Sunday Times* Desmond Shawe-Taylor wrote that, faced with a choice between four different performances of this work in as many months, 'the casting of Marguerite had decided me' and continued: 'Mr Pritchard had engaged for this role our Covent Garden *Figaro* Countess, Kiri Te Kanawa, who possesses as pure, smooth and beautiful a stream of soprano tone, very forwardly produced, as is now to be heard anywhere. Although traces of artistic and technical immaturity are still to be found in her work, there are few singers before the public whose appearances I look forward to so eagerly; and her Marguerite, granted a certain want of familiarity with the French idiom and language, was indeed exquisite.'

But no staged performances of *The Damnation of Faust* were envisaged and Kiri remained a universally approved and applauded soprano who still had only one major operatic role (not including Desdemona) in her repertoire. Such a state of affairs could hardly be allowed to continue. Fortunately, Kiri had recently discovered another source of help to augment that she obtained from Vera Rozsa and her coaches on the music staff at Covent Garden. This was a warm, cheerful and energetic lady named Jean Mallandaine, who had studied the piano at the Royal Academy of Music with accompaniment as her speciality; she had done a certain amount of coaching of students at the London Opera Centre while Kiri was there and had occasionally worked with her. Jean Mallandaine remembers now: 'They all talked about this girl from New Zealand with the marvellous voice who never went to any classes or turned up for any coaching. Eventually she came my way and we got on very well: I didn't have a problem. I'd see her the day before and say, "Remember you're with me at eleven tomorrow – will you remember?" And she'd say, "Oh yes, I'll remember," and would dutifully turn up. But she didn't like the schoolroom approach and I think she was very unhappy and unsettled when she first came to London. I think at that stage it had all happened without her deciding whether she wanted to do it, and she was always rushing off to buy clothes and accumulating parking tickets. The trouble was that at the Centre so few people seemed to want to make her feel at home or get the best out of her.

In institutions like that if you're not like everyone else, they don't want to know. The others had learned crotchets and quavers and here was this girl, who hadn't prepared anything, being given major roles.'

After the Opera Centre Jean Mallandaine had been working as a freelance coach and also on the music staff of Glyndebourne Festival Opera during the summer seasons. She had rather lost touch with Kiri but one day in 1972: 'She called me out of the blue and asked if I would help her. So I used to go down to Esher. At first she found she could only work in short spasms of about half an hour before saying, "Let's go and get something nice for lunch," or else remember that she had to go to a dress shop for something she wanted. Then we'd come back and do some more work. I'd set aside a day – it's no good fighting a person's approach – it's much better to compromise.' Eventually she and Kiri worked out a scheme because, 'With Kiri you really had to go from the basics. I don't think she liked learning or was very good at learning the basic stuff on her own. She works from the sound rather than the sight of something on the page, because she doesn't actually sight-read music very well. She's not slow but is reluctant to make a start on anything new, so there's that initial laziness to get over. On the other hand, she has a photographic memory as well as an extremely good aural memory. So things tend always to be a little bit last-minute; but I think she likes and needs that kind of pressure.'

The system that Jean evolved was to make special tapes from which Kiri could learn a new role. 'I would record the role, with a skeleton accompaniment, playing her notes on the piano, so she could be in her hotel room, or wherever, and could get it into her head that way. When she went to Italy Desmond would send the tapes out to her. It was very funny: I would put little messages on the tape as well as the notes – tell her a joke or something to keep it lively. I remember once saying, "When you've learned this duet, then on the other side of the tape I've put the other singers' lines, so you can practise singing against them." When she came back and we were rehearsing together, as she reached the point where the music finished on the first side, she said, returning the joke, "When you have learned this duet etc" – she'd learned precisely what I'd said as well as the notes!'

In addition to making tapes Jean would give Kiri sustained coaching to supplement her lessons with Vera Rozsa. Here the approach was, 'When we got past the notes we would work on more important things like presentation, interpretation, language and diction. Kiri has the advantage of one hundred per cent confidence in her voice and she always has had as long as I've known her. She never seems to worry about things going wrong vocally. I've never heard her say, "I can't possibly do that" as so many singers will. Vera's work with her was much more on the technical side of the voice, though helping a great deal interpretatively as well. In fact to begin with, I found it very helpful to go with Kiri to the lessons with Vera and hear what Vera did, so that afterwards I'd be able to tell her when we were working together, "That wasn't what you did with Vera," and then she'd recall it, which was most helpful. The coaching at that stage was pretty vital really, because Kiri just had to find a way of learning new roles quickly; she'd suddenly become famous as the Countess, but still had no repertoire.'

After completing her Fellowship study period, Kiri's first engagement in February on return from Italy was to record Mozart's beautiful, but incomplete Mass in C minor, K.427 for EMI. This had been the cause of yet another tape being sent to Italy by Jean. 'Des rang saying Kiri was in a panic about it and could I make one straight away!' This was an important recording for her, with Raymond Leppard conducting the New Philharmonia, and Ileana Cotrubas, Werner Krenn and Hans Sotin as her fellow soloists. At that stage she was still in the process of discovering a recording technique. '*Parsifal* was the first major thing I was involved in. I hadn't recorded earlier from my own choice, as I thought if I was going to record I should do it very well or not at all. I was pleased with the Decca sound for *Parsifal*, but I still hadn't got it quite right. There's a special technique for singing into the microphone: for the Philips set of Mozart church music with Colin Davis I was trying too hard and the voice wasn't coming through – really they need to invent a special microphone to allow for it. You have to manage to come through on the plastic as if they're hearing you in the concert hall – it's very difficult. The *C minor Mass* seemed to come out better, though it still isn't absolutely right.' *Gramophone*'s critic, Trevor Harvey, was however well pleased with the result, writing: 'Earlier these works were never performed in the concert hall (and for that matter are still seldom heard). One reason is that they demand coloratura singers (the ladies at any rate) of the greatest virtuosity, and such rare birds are expensive. Which brings me now to the present performance, for with Ileana Cotrubas and Kiri Te Kanawa you can hardly go wrong. Miss Cotrubas's purity of line, her technique (including admirable trills) are applied to real artistry; and, though both are billed as sopranos, Miss Te Kanawa has a different, rather richer, quality that makes just enough contrast when they are in duet.' Kiri did not, and does not, have any cause for dissatisfaction: it remains a glorious recording, one that displays her vocal quality to admirable effect and is a constant pleasure to hear.

So began an unprecedentedly busy year in which the diary sheets kept for her by Basil Horsfield recorded no fewer than one hundred and one separate engagements, ranging from 'covering' at Covent Garden to performing there, from concerts to recordings to television programmes. Kiri may still have been on a relatively lowly-salaried contract but from the point of view of output at least, the big time was undoubtedly beginning to arrive. The small-time part of her contractual obligations at the Royal Opera House began early in the year: another series of Flower Maidens in *Parsifal*, followed by Priestesses in *Aida*, during March and April.

One engagement provided some light relief, appropriately perhaps, on 1 April at the London Palladium. This was a charity gala in aid of the Army Benevolent Fund and sponsored by the Variety Club of Great Britain, called 'Fall in the Stars'. This was a well-mixed evening in which the participants included such household names as Ronnie Corbett, Rachel Roberts, Alfred Marks, Beryl Reid, Fenella Fielding, Jimmy Tarbuck, Geraint Evans, Kiri and, above all, as the gala's moving spirit, Harry Secombe, that irrepressible Welsh comedian with the magnificent tenor voice. Kiri and Geraint joined him for an item towards the end of the programme, and the sense of fun of all three was conspicuously in evidence. Secombe was already a good friend of hers, for Kiri had by now appeared on several of his television programmes – as she continues to do – and enormously enjoyed working with him. (In 1981, when he appeared on Thames Television's *This Is Your Life* programme about Kiri on Christmas Day, Sir Harry, as he was by then, told Eamonn Andrews: 'I've got my own special name for her too. When I first met her I thought it might be a bit intimidating to appear with a Covent Garden opera singer, and I had a bit of trouble pronouncing her name. So she told me, "Just call me tin knickers!" and far from being intimidating, she turned out to be a beautiful and talented girl with a really lovely sense of humour.') The gala was attended by Princess Margaret, played to a full house and was a great success. It also provided a cheerful diversion before the hard and serious work that lay ahead.

Straight after Covent Garden's revivals of *Parsifal* and *Aida* there came, in April, a new production of Mozart's *Don Giovanni* for which, as in the 1971 *The Marriage of Figaro*, John Copley was producer and Stefanos Lazaridis the designer. Kiri was not scheduled to sing in the opening series nor in the new production's first revival in November though, as it turned out, November was in fact when she made her stage debut in the role of Elvira. In April she was 'covering' Elvira, which was sung by the South African soprano Wendy Fine; but more importantly Kiri had been cast by Colin Davis to sing the role in his new recording of the opera for Philips, which was to be made during May at Watford Town Hall, north of London. Such are the vagaries of the record industry that this recording, though conducted by Colin Davis and using the orchestra and chorus of the Royal Opera House, had an almost totally different cast from the one which had sung in the new production there the previous month: only Stuart Burrows as Don Ottavio and John Constable playing the harpsichord continuo were common to both production and recording. Moreover, when Kiri did in fact sing in the Covent Garden production in November, it was still only Burrows and herself who had sung their roles on the recording, which by then had just been released; Richard Van Allan, who had recorded Masetto in May, was now singing Leporello.

The cast for the Philips recording had the Swedish baritone Ingvar Wixell as Don Giovanni, the black American soprano Martina Arroyo as Donna Anna, the Italians Mirella Freni, Wladimiro Ganzarolli, and Luigi Roni as Zerlina, Leporello, and the Commenddatore respectively, and Welsh Stuart Burrows and Maori Kiri as Ottavio and Elvira, along with English Richard Van Allan as Masetto. The sessions at Watford went well, though Kiri now regards it as strange, and rather unfortunate, that she recorded the complex role of Elvira before she actually sang it on stage. She was still trying to discover a cast-iron recording technique: 'Microphone technique is so vital – the microphone, for example, won't take "bumps", and there are plenty of those in Elvira's music. Placido Domingo, for instance, has the most wonderful microphone technique; I don't know how he does it, but on records too he always, without exception, produces a wonderful sound.' Nevertheless Colin Davis recalls Kiri 'working incredibly hard on Elvira', and he was well pleased with her results.

Philips issued the recording in November coinciding, as it turned out, with Kiri's Covent Garden debut in the role. Good as her performance on record is, it does not represent Kiri's finished view of the role: that may be found on the much more recent CBS recording of *Don Giovanni*, conducted by Lorin Maazel with Ruggero Raimondi in the title role, which came as a by-product of Joseph Losey's remarkable film of the opera. But sadly neither the Philips nor the CBS recording truly captures the full beauty of Kiri's voice nor the bloom of her tone in this role, which one hears when she sings it in the opera house. In *Gramophone* the Philips set was reviewed by John Warrack who, having noted the contrast between Kiri's performance and Martina Arroyo's grandly dramatic Donna Anna, continued: 'Sweet, light and precise of voice, she touches charmingly upon the essence of many passages; and it is excellent to have "Mi tradì" for once sung with proper attention to the words, that it is to say with at least as much inward regret and sadness as fury against Giovanni. Yet though here, and in "Ah, che mi dice mai", she is delightful, she makes too little of "Ah, fuggi"; and in general she seems wary of throwing herself into a full understanding of Elvira's fraught, desperate and half-violent character, as well as her wounded nature.'

She would come far nearer to it in November when she rehearsed John Copley's production, but in May she had learned her role for the recording, but not yet for the opera. As Harold Rosenthal remarked when reviewing this recording in the January 1974 issue of *Opera* (which also contained a 'rave' review of her Covent Garden performance of the role from Alan Blyth, plus her photograph in Elvira's costume on the cover) 'Kiri Te Kanawa's Elvira is promising, but the recording engineers do not seem to have succeeded in capturing the natural beauty of her voice. Playing the set again after her recent triumphant Elvira at Covent Garden, I must say that I wish she could have recorded this role next summer instead of last – then we might have had one of the finest Elviras on record.'

Following the recording sessions for *Don Giovanni*, and just before rehearsals began for Covent Garden's new production of *Carmen*, something rather exciting happened. For some little time 'Bill' Barrett, and others who had been connected with Kiri's early progress and development in New Zealand, had been urging the Government there that it might be fitting to recognize her achievements on behalf of her country by putting forward her name for an honour. The result was that on 1 June 1973 a cable was sent 'Priority' from Wellington to Mrs K. J. Park in Esher saying: 'Personal: I have much pleasure in informing you that the Queen has been graciously pleased on the occasion of Her Majesty's birthday to confer upon you the honour of Officer of the Civil Division of the Most Excellent Order of the British Empire – stop – Please accept my warm congratulations – stop – Official announcement will be made here tomorrow (Saturday) morning. Denis

Blundell Governor General.' Thus the following day, Kiri's name –
as Mrs D. Park – duly appeared in the New Zealand section of the
Queen's Birthday Honours list, as an OBE, and another telegram
of congratulation arrived from Wellington, this time from the
Prime Minister, Norman Kirk. Kiri was absolutely delighted to
receive what she now laughingly describes as 'my obe', especially
at the young age of twenty-nine. But what pleased her most was that
in the same list her original teacher, Sister Mary Leo, was appointed
a Dame Commander of the British Empire, thus henceforth to be
known as Dame Sister Mary Leo. Needless to say, pupil and teacher
exchanged letters of congratulation, and equally needless to say the
New Zealand press and its readers were delighted. The *New Zealand
Herald* in an editorial on 2 June wrote: 'Double pleasure will be felt
in the harmonious coincidence that places Sister Mary Leo and one
of her most successful pupils, Miss Kiri Te Kanawa (Mrs Park), on
the same list. Sister Mary Leo, now a DBE, has a gift of teaching and
a stamp of personality that have made her as fine a singing teacher
as New Zealand has known; Miss Te Kanawa, a young OBE, has
achieved much and could have a whole career in front of her.' Kiri,
later in the summer, was invested with her honour by the Queen
at Buckingham Palace. Desmond accompanied her there, and Kiri
was thrilled and amazed to discover that the Queen had remembered
her from the time they had met in Dunedin in 1970.

Her next operatic assignment was the role of Micaela in Covent
Garden's new production of *Carmen*, which opened with a gala
performance, attended by the Queen Mother, on 4 July. This was
conducted by Sir Georg Solti, the Royal Opera's former Music
Director who, after his earlier reservations, was now a firm supporter
of Kiri's work. She was working with a truly top-flight international
group: Carmen was sung by the black American mezzo-soprano
Shirley Verrett, the tenor Placido Domingo, fast rising to the summit,
was Don José, and Escamillo was taken by the exciting Belgian
bass-baritone, José Van Dam. This fine cast was originally to have
been directed by Franco Zeffirelli but the distinguished Italian
had, sadly, withdrawn a few months earlier and Michael Geliot,

then Artistic Director of Welsh National Opera, had the not-altogether-enviable task of taking over a prestigious production at relatively very short notice.

For the most part Kiri greatly enjoyed the rehearsal period. 'I loved working with Solti, Shirley Verrett and, above all, Domingo was fantastic. But I did have one row with Michael Geliot. One boiling hot day at London Opera Centre he sat the cast and chorus down and told us the story of Carmen, which we'd already read and gone through. Then he asked me to sing my big Act 3 aria to the whole chorus. I was never so embarrassed, so sick with nerves at having to get up and sing like that to the chorus. I thought I'd get up the chorus's backs, and they're the one group of people you want behind you to support you. I don't know why he wanted me to do it, but I did my usual bitchy thing and sang it an octave down. He was absolutely furious with me, and said things about people who couldn't do their job properly. So I went into my dream world – what Des calls "getting my Maori up" – and turned off. There was no point in losing my temper: the only way to fight back is to do your job really well, and from then on that's what I tried to do.'

The resulting production, though perfectly acceptable and attractive to look at in Jenny Beavan and David Fielding's working, rather than travel-poster, Seville sets, was not perhaps quite the coup de théâtre that people had been expecting and hoping for, given the quality of the forces involved. Possibly it wasn't helped by the decision to use Fritz Oeser's edition of Bizet's score, which claims to return to the composer's original intentions and uses spoken dialogue rather than the sung recitatives that Bizet's contemporary Guiraud wrote. Whereas the dialogue had worked well in English National Opera's English language performances at the Coliseum, they came over less happily at Covent Garden, spoken by a cast of which only one member, José Van Dam, was naturally a French-speaker. There was thus a wide variety of accents on display which caused me, writing at the time in *The Tatler*, to refer to what 'sounded like a Berlitz conversation class'. Certainly the dialogue was somewhat stilted. Nevertheless, Kiri looked most attractive as

José's original girl-friend, a healthy, wholesome country girl, whom he deserts for the fatal eroticism of the gypsy Carmen, superbly and subtly portrayed by Shirley Verrett. Moreover Kiri sang both her arias with great musicality and her habitual creamy tone and, if she sounded less confident in her dialogue, she moved around the stage with assurance.

For the most part she received approving notices in the press. In *The Times* Stanley Sadie wrote: 'The two outstanding performances come from Kiri Te Kanawa and José Van Dam. Miss Te Kanawa brings an aptly warm personality, and a warm fresh voice to match, to Micaela's music; the Act 1 song was full of felicities in timing, the third-act plea to José open, sincere and very touching.' In the *Sunday Times* Desmond Shawe-Taylor noted that, 'Kiri Te Kanawa brought her full, sweet soprano to Micaela's music, and made of her a more natural and positive character than usual.' But there were others, such as Martin Cooper in the *Daily Telegraph* and Harold Rosenthal in *Opera*, who felt that the role did not suit her. Rosenthal wrote: 'Kiri Te Kanawa sang with a lovely creamy tone as Micaela, but seemed temperamentally not at home in Seville – she was a very genteel village girl!' Maybe he was right; certainly, although Kiri sang the role in Covent Garden's revival the following year and recorded it for Decca (again with Solti conducting, Domingo as José and Van Dam as Escamillo, though with Tatiana Troyanos now singing Carmen) at the end of 1975, she has not returned to it since then and has no plans to do so. This seems rather a shame: temperamentally Micaela's is a more docile part (as well as being only a second soprano role) than Kiri's current favourites of Elvira, Fiordiligi and, perhaps above all, Arabella, but she nonetheless has much to offer the role.

Immediately after the first night of *Carmen* Kiri had to go down to Sussex, to Glyndebourne, to start rehearsing the Countess in Peter Hall's new production of Mozart's *The Marriage of Figaro*. Sadly for her, as she was in the second cast which took over in the production half-way through its run, she was not actually rehearsed in the role by Hall himself. 'His assistant, Adrian Slack, took my rehearsals, and I think I only did one with Peter Hall, at the end of the run, before the special performance we did for Southern Television. I did go down on the opening night to see how his production looked, with Elizabeth Harwood then singing the Countess, but I greatly regret not yet doing a production from scratch with Peter Hall – perhaps one day it will happen. Sometimes singers say on a first night, "Thank God the producer will be gone by tomorrow, and then we can get on with the performances" – but that isn't the case with him.'

Nevertheless she immensely enjoyed the time she spent at Glyndebourne. 'It was one of the great enjoyments of my life – I loved the people there, even though I'd auditioned for them for *La Calisto* in the 1960s and they'd never used me – that was all in the past. But though there was a certain amount of backbiting and petty jealousy amongst the singers, I was as happy as a lark and got on extremely well with everyone. I'd love to go back there one day but it's difficult: it takes such a long time to do things the way they do at Glyndebourne. These days I'd really prefer to take three months off altogether – unpaid – and spend the time with my family.'

Her Glyndebourne Countess was in fact an enormous success, and one that she repeated there the following year. In 1973's cast were the Norwegian Knut Skram as Figaro, Benjamin Luxon as the Count, Ileana Cotrubas, followed by the Swedish soprano Britta Möllerström as Susanna, and Frederica von Stade as an incomparably perfect Cherubino. I was lucky enough to see a performance in August at which Kiri sang the Countess and Cotrubas took Susanna. In the much smaller house at Glyndebourne – in Peter Hall's exquisitely human production which truly came across as taking place within a 'family and during one hectic day, as Beaumarchais's original play intended – Kiri's Countess seemed flawless. Not only did she sing magnificently and look quite stunningly beautiful, but I found this Rosina to be a much more complete and thus real, character. This Countess was more fully in command and, though unhappy, displayed far greater resource and mettle as the wronged wife, nonetheless confident of ultimate victory over her errant husband, than in those Covent Garden performances eighteen months earlier, memorably heartfelt though they had been. Moreover, as Harold Rosenthal wrote later in the Festival issue of *Opera*: 'She seemed more of a flesh-and-blood character as the Countess than she has so far been at Covent Garden. Looking as lovely as ever, and reacting more than somewhat to the advances of Cherubino, this Countess certainly behaved in a manner that would have rightly aroused the Count's jealousy.' In sum, she seemed a genuinely aristocratic, highly attractive young wife, in whose feelings one could totally believe: this was *dramma per musica* at a high level.

These same qualities came vividly across in the Southern Television performance, produced by Humphrey Burton and directed by David Heather. It would be most rewarding to see that on television once again: it is so much more persuasive an interpretation of the opera than the television version made by Unitel in 1976, directed by Jean-Pierre Ponnelle and conducted by Karl Böhm, in which Kiri again took the role of the Countess, and which comes over as self-conscious and fussy when compared with the clarity and directness of Peter Hall's Glyndebourne staging.

Following the Glyndebourne season and the television recording of *Figaro* came a much needed holiday until the middle of September. Kiri's main engagement of the autumn at Covent Garden was to be her debut in the role of Amelia in Verdi's *Simone Boccanegra*. This was a role which she had been studying and preparing for some time, having begun to learn it in San Francisco the previous year: she had gone there armed with scores and tapes of *Boccanegra*. It hadn't taken her long to discover that Amelia's music lay absolutely right for her voice, and by the time that rehearsals began, helped by lessons with Vera Rozsa, coaching with Jean Mallandaine, and further coaching at Covent Garden from the revival's conductor, John Matheson, Kiri had done her homework very thoroughly indeed.

In what might perhaps have proved a routine revival, by one of Covent Garden's staff producers, of Tito Gobbi's originally somewhat pedestrian and now eight-year-old production, Kiri created a sensation, and this despite the presence of Boris Christoff singing Jacopo Fiesco, Amelia's unrecognized grandfather, and Peter Glossop as her father, the Doge Boccanegra. On stage she looked quite wonderfully assured, poised and beautiful in her medieval dress, her face radiating the sheer joy of singing Verdi's beautiful music in that superb first act aria 'Come in quest'ora bruna' as Amelia muses on the beauty of the sky and sea, while the orchestra echo that beauty in the lower strings with a quite exquisite accompaniment; it was a deeply moving experience. In the finale of the great Council Chamber scene at the end of Act 1, and also in the magnificent trio for Amelia, her lover Adorno, and Boccanegra at the close of Act 2, Kiri's voice soared effortlessly distinct from the other singers and the orchestral accompaniment. It was unforgettable Verdian singing and totally remarkable for a soprano not yet thirty.

Predictably the press were ecstatic. Never before had she received such unanimously enthusiastic notices in London and never had they been more richly deserved. 'A Thrilling Soprano' was *The Times*'s headline above Stanley Sadie's review which accorded 'pride of place' to Kiri and continued: 'She lives the role: her singing is coloured by love, anxiety, terror, or whatever other emotion possesses her; and her movement on the stage is supple and full of life and feeling. Add to all that the unfair advantage of Miss Te Kanawa's exceptional physical beauty, and you have a rare and marvellous impersonation.' Similar enthusiasm was expressed by Andrew Porter in the *Financial Times*, who in his opening paragraph stated: 'Particularly beautiful was the Amelia of Kiri Te Kanawa,' went on to compare her 'ravishing' singing of the role with the New York Metropolitan's first Amelia, Maria Müller, and closed a lengthy and detailed appraisal of her performance with these words: 'She looked beautiful, she acted well, and fully characterized both the personage and the music. It is a rare pleasure to be able to praise the interpreter of a Verdian heroine without any reservations whatever.' In case she was still not satisfied, Harold Rosenthal took up the chorus in the December issue of *Opera* and described her performance as 'The revelation of the evening ... Here was Verdi soprano singing on the highest level.' Having gone on to applaud her 'amazing breath control and technique' he concluded: 'She looked as ravishing as she sounded and succeeded in bringing to life a character that in all previous *Boccanegra* performances I have found dull and very much a cardboard figure.' Funnily enough, this had also been Kiri's own initial reaction: she told Robert Jacobson of *Opera News* the following year, 'I hated Amelia until I did it. I felt it an impossible task with such a difficult opera, and a not-so-good production.'

Now that she had sung Amelia, Kiri, and Vera Rozsa equally, could feel delighted by such an unparalleled and unqualified success; but there was no question of their sitting back and simply enjoying it. The first revival of the April production of *Don Giovanni* was to open on 28 November – less than three weeks after the final performances of *Boccanegra* – and the Italian soprano Margherita Rinaldi, cast to sing Elvira, had cancelled all her performances because she was pregnant. Not until the end of October was Kiri formally engaged to replace her and by then the *Boccanegra* was already well under way. She recalls: 'Immediately after opening in *Boccanegra* came a telephone call saying someone had cancelled Elvira. I had about three weeks' notice to learn it properly and I didn't yet know anyone else's part: for the recording I'd only really learned Elvira's, which is all right for recording sessions, but for a stage performance it makes it very very hard if you don't know everyone else's part too. Fortunately I was singing with Margaret Price, whom I adored, as Donna Anna and we all got on enormously well.'

Indeed most of the cast were singers whom Kiri already knew and liked: Richard Van Allan as Leporello, Ryland Davies as Ottavio, Teresa Cahill and Robert Lloyd as Zerlina and Masetto, with John Copley the producer and Colin Davis conducting, so she was certainly among friends and on home ground. One stranger was Cesare Siepi, the distinguished Italian bass who was singing Giovanni. 'He kept saying, "Where's Kanawa" – he thought I was Japanese – but once we'd overcome that we got on splendidly!' Fortunately, too, she felt an immediate rapport with John Copley and Stefanos Lazaridis's somewhat controversial production, set amongst tubular rods on a steeply raked stage (this was replaced during Covent Garden's Mozart Festival in the summer of 1981 by Peter Wood's more neutral and less stimulating staging).

'I loved that production: it gave me the best Elvira I've ever had a chance to express – I discovered the character in it. There is no other production that I've been in since that expresses the Elvira I want to do in the way that this one did.' Kiri felt the way she took the role that first time in London was exactly right, and says of Elvira's character: 'Basically she's a rampant, raving hot-pants – but only for Don Giovanni. She isn't hot-pants for anyone else, just terribly in love with Giovanni to whom, she reckoned, she'd been married for three days before the opera starts. There just are some women who stand up and you think they're on heat all the time: I feel Elvira was that type of woman – her whole physique pulsated – she'd been ruled by her sex-life but nevertheless was a one-man woman. At the end of the opera, after Giovanni has gone to hell, she says she's going to enter a convent. She means it – and she'll stay there, because there's no one left for her to love.' Kiri sees Elvira's character in strong contrast to Donna Anna's far more rigid and conventional mould, but has thought of trying that role too. 'I'd like to make her a character as well, but I think I'd put too much of Elvira into her, and for that reason Des has always asked me to promise I'll never do Donna Anna.'

Despite the shortness of notice that she was to sing Elvira at Covent Garden or perhaps because of it –it really made her buckle down and concentrate on the role – her performance was another triumph. There was no feeling in it of a young soprano tentatively tackling a major Mozartean role for the very first time, nor of finding her way into the character. This was a finished, fully-considered interpretation, which portrayed Elvira essentially and convincingly, as Kiri saw her. The effect was gripping. Once again she was acclaimed by the press. William Mann's notice in *The Times* was headlined: 'Ladies take almost all of the honours' and described Kiri's characterization of Elvira as 'a tigress in desolation, because pining for

[126]

affection, and clinging pathetically to it after every deception'. Peter Stadlen's review in the *Daily Telegraph* was headlined: 'Fresh Elvira of Kiri Te Kanawa' and found, 'There was something delightfully fresh and personal about Miss Te Kanawa's Elvira. She was not the crushed victim that is apt to render one uneasy, but a defiant, attractive young woman singing to herself or addressing her fugitive lover with engaging directness and in melodies of authentic double meaning, musical and amorous.' In the *Financial Times* Andrew Porter once again approved, writing that her 'first Elvira was a glowing and passionate performance, securely and eloquently voiced, romantically phrased'.

Best of all perhaps was Alan Blyth's appraisal in January's issue of *Opera* for, having in the past chided Kiri for her lack of attention to words and want of characterization, he now wrote: 'None was more arresting than Kiri Te Kanawa's Elvira. This artist, no doubt with Mr Copley's unflagging help, has transformed herself from negative to very positive in two years. Her frenzied, distraught portrayal delivered in Italian that was almost uncomfortably clear in projection, commanded the stage. The recitative to "Mi tradì", accompanied with tormented sweetness by Mr Davis, was just its most telling aspect, and the aria itself showed the myriad colours in [her] rich, succulent voice. Once or twice she seemed to be trying just too hard to bury the placid image. Otherwise this was the finest Elvira since Schwarzkopf and Jurinac were in their prime (and I do not forget Zylis-Gara's noble performance).'

The rest of the run was not without its hazards, however, and before one performance Kiri succumbed to 'flu and was forced to cancel – something she does extremely rarely and only if positively forbidden to sing by her doctor. The result at that performance was that Teresa Cahill switched from Zerlina to Elvira and Anne Pashley gallantly took on Zerlina at three hours' notice. Despite her great success and enjoyment of the role, Kiri was relieved when *Don Giovanni*'s run of performances ended and she and Desmond could get away on holiday over Christmas and New Year. 1973 had been a hectic, desperately hard-working year for her, though an enormously successful one. It was crowned on 31 December when New Zealand's *Dominion* newspaper awarded her the honour of 'New Zealander of the Year'. The paper's music critic, Russell Bond, wrote: 'Without doubt she has arrived. New Zealand can well be proud of her. To her voice of lovely quality she adds beauty of face and figure. Now she can be acclaimed as a star of international status.' This was true, and with her debut at New York's Metropolitan Opera to come, unexpectedly, in less than two months' time, Kiri's international status was about to be underlined and enlarged.

'Among the three or four outstanding singers in the world and the possessor of the loveliest voice of them all.' A picture to support Bernard Levin's verdict in 1976.

As Fiordiligi in Jean-Pierre Ponnelle's production of Mozart's *Cosi fan tutte* at the Paris Opéra in 1976.

Opposite:
Above: At home in Esher, 1976.

Below: Cobber, Kiri's constant companion.

Kiri and Desmond with their daughter Toni, aged two.

Below: Audiences at Esher were less easily impressed than those at Covent Garden.

Above: A well-earned
rest for Kiri as the
Countess and for
Mirella Freni as
Suzanna during the
filming of Unitel's
production of Mozart's
The Marriage of Figaro at
Shepperton Studios, 1976.

Right: Kiri's first
Arabella, in the title role
of Strauss's opera, at
Covent Garden, 1977.

Left: Rehearsing the role of Rosalinde in Strauss's *Die Fledermaus,* with Hermann Prey as her husband Gabriel von Eisenstein, for Covent Garden's new production at the very end of 1977.

Below: With the same production's conductor, Zubin Mehta, during rehearsals.

Opposite: As Violetta, with Heather Begg as Flora, in John Copley's new production of Verdi's *La Traviata* at the Sydney Opera House, 1978.

Opposite:Below: Discussing her role as Donna Elvira with director Joseph Losey during filming of Mozart's *Don Giovanni,* near Vicenza, 1978.

Singing 'Mi Tradi' in the same film.

Above: Rehearsing for a concert in Salzburg with Claudio Abbado conducting the Vienna Philharmonic Orchestra in 1979, the score for Mozart's 'Exsultate Jubilate' to hand.

Left: Getting the goat to the Garden: a 'party guest' appearance with Sally from Chessington Zoo at a gala performance of Johann Strauss's *Die Fledermaus* in the presence of HM Queen Elizabeth the Queen Mother at the Royal Opera House, 1980.

As Pamina, with Stuart Burrows as Tamino, in Covent Garden's production of Mozart's *The Magic Flute*, 1980.

Above: Playing golf for the BBC against Placido Domingo at Wentworth in 1980. Kiri's caddy is Bernard Levin, Placido's Sir John Tooley.

Right: Well on course.

With Dame Joan Sutherland (*centre*) and Angela Lansbury during recording sessions for John Gay's *The Beggar's Opera* in London, 1981.

Opposite:
Above: Discussing the recording of Mozart's *The Marriage of Figaro* with Sir Georg Solti at Kingsway Hall, London, 1981.

Below: With Frederica von Stade and Thomas Allen during the same recording sessions.

Producer Peter Wood (*back to camera*) and conductor Sir Colin Davis rehearsing Kiri and Ruggero Raimondi for Covent Garden's new production of Mozart's *Don Giovanni*, 1981.

As Donna Elvira in the same production.

The bright seraph. Kiri singing Handel's 'Let the Bright Seraphim' at the marriage of HRH the Prince of Wales to the Lady Diana Spencer at St Paul's cathedral, London in 1981. Sir Colin Davis is seated left and Sir David Willcocks is conducting the Bach Choir.

With Desmond, Toni and Thomas at Thames Television's recording of *This Is Your Life*, shown on Christmas Day 1981. Visible in the background are Richard Baker and Stuart Burrows.

An enormous personal success: Kiri's first *Tosca*, in the title role of a new production of Puccini's work at the Paris Opéra, 1982.

10

New York and Paris

KIRI HAD DECIDED to arrive in New York in plenty of time for her debut as Desdemona in Verdi's *Otello* at the Metropolitan Opera. Her first performance wasn't scheduled to take place until 7 March, the sixth of *Otello*'s run; but Kiri, on Basil's advice, had decided to be there from the beginning of the rehearsal period and to 'cover' Teresa Stratas's performances as Desdemona, so that when her turn came to sing the role she would know all about the production and be able to find her way around the Met's enormous stage. One reason for this lengthy preparation period was that she was determined to prove to Covent Garden that she could succeed in a major role at another major opera house before she sang it there. Kiri was due to sing Desdemona at the Royal Opera House in May and her plan to sing it at the Met first had been vigorously opposed. 'Covent Garden were totally against it. They all tried to stop me and said I should do everything for the first time at Covent Garden, as that was my home base and where I had my contract. Even Colin Davis was against it – it was one of the very few occasions when I displeased him. He said the audience in New York would kill me – I think he was trying to over-protect me. But I was determined to do it and nothing was going to stop me: I just had to go out into the big cold world. I wasn't covering any roles at Covent Garden, except Elvira in *Don Giovanni*, so all I had to do was to ask for leave.'

The result of this was that Kiri arrived in New York, entirely alone, on 28 January 1974. Desmond, Vera, Basil and other friends were due to arrive in time for her first night but till March there were just Sam Niefeld and the New Zealand Consulate to look after her. The Consul-General, Paul Cotton, and his wife gave a reception in Kiri's honour a week after her arrival, which was comforting. Even better, in view of her solo status in the city, they provided Kiri with a young New Zealand girl called Rosanne to stay and keep her company in the flat she had taken on West End Avenue, about ten blocks from the Lincoln Center and the opera house.

The opening performance of *Otello*, with Jon Vickers in the title role, Teresa Stratas as Desdemona and Thomas Stewart as Iago, conducted by James Levine was on 9 February, a Saturday matinée, one of the series that were radio broadcast live from the Met nationwide. Kiri duly attended rehearsals and had coaching sessions to refresh her memory of the music, for it was nearly two years since she had sung Desdemona with Scottish Opera. But as Teresa Stratas was singing the opening performances Kiri did not in fact get a chance actually to rehearse the opera on-stage and thus become acquainted with Franco Zeffirelli's large-scale, realistic, highly-detailed, and complex production. This wouldn't have greatly mattered – there was still plenty of time before her 7 March debut – had not Teresa Stratas, who had previously cancelled one rehearsal, suddenly fallen ill on Friday, 8 February. All through that day Kiri was put on notice of having to replace her at the opening the following afternoon. She explains, 'Sam Niefeld and I told the Met we had to know, one way or the other, by nine o'clock on Friday night. I felt I was being left absolutely high and dry. I tried to phone Des in London, but he'd gone away for the weekend, and I couldn't find Basil either. Then at nine they rang and said: "It's fine – Stratas is going to do it." It was a great relief; I went straight to bed and had my best night's sleep since I'd arrived in New York. Then, next morning, I'd just got up when the phone rang at ten. I said, jokingly, to Rosanne: "If it's the Met, tell them I'm out!" It was and she did. So the Met told her that when I got in I should phone them very urgently – there was an emergency. Of course I rang straight back and they told me that Stratas had cancelled and that I should get down there immediately. I rang up Sam and said, "I've got a funny feeling I'm going to be on," had a steak, then set off for the Met.' It was snowing, so she took a cab. 'The driver didn't seem to know where the Met was and it took an hour to go ten blocks. When I arrived Jon Vickers, James Levine and the stage director, Fabrizio Melano, had a rehearsal all lined up to walk me through the production on-set. Of course I wasn't prepared – nobody's ever prepared for a shock – and I was absolutely terrified.'

Fortunately for Kiri she had a singer of Vickers's experience and consideration as her Otello. As he later explained to Michael Owen of the *Evening Standard* in London: 'We did conspire a bit before Kiri came in. The conductor, the producer and myself decided to rehearse the whole opera with her. The Met debut is a very frightening experience. The first time you come in everybody says, "Who is this?" I've been through all these things, so I tried to make a bit of a fuss of her to let her know she was among friends.' In the same article Kiri observed, 'Jon was marvellous: he got me through it. When I went in for that first rehearsal he said, "Hi Kiri, how are you?" and from then on they were all very sweet to me. But I have never been so nervous. I trembled until the end of the fourth act. I survived by pure concentration. The *relief* at the end of it! Jon said I was high as a kite.'

As far as the audience were concerned, however, it was not relief but boundless enthusiasm they felt at the final curtain. As the critic Allen Hughes wrote in the *New York Times* on the following Monday: 'It was past six o'clock at the Metropolitan Opera on Saturday afternoon and time for everyone to clear out so that the house could be gotten ready for the evening performance, but most of the matinée audience was reluctant to leave. What it wanted was to register its cheering approval of the principals in the splendid performance of Verdi's *Otello* that had just ended. And one principal was a particular source of interest. That was Kiri Te Kanawa, a New Zealand-born soprano who, with a few hours' notice, had made her Metropolitan debut in the part of Desdemona . . . Miss Te Kanawa won the audience from the very beginning and did not lose it. Her voice had a lovely fresh sound, her vocal production was smooth, her singing was eloquent and her acting was touching and invariably believable. She is slim and attractive, and the impression she made as Desdemona was satisfying in every way.'

In addition to the audience in the opera house, whom Kiri felt had given her a great opportunity to do well by making her feel they were on her side, there were literally millions who had listened on the radio and were similarly excited. One radio listener was *Opera*'s critic in New York, George Movshon, who was 'immediately won over by the limpid, innately musical singing she gave us' and made sure to be present on 7 March when Kiri sang again opposite James McCracken: 'She is a major addition to the roster and can look forward to a big American career.' In San Francisco Kiri has a great friend, a consultant anaesthetist named Jason Soifer, whom she had met through mutual friends during her first visit to the city in 1972. She explains 'Jason was driving his car in the hills above San Francisco when he heard the announcement on the radio, and came to a crashing halt. The radio announcer was Milton Cross, who died shortly afterwards, and having announced "This is the Metropolitan Opera" he then had great difficulty pronouncing my name! Jason just sat there in the mountains listening to his car radio for the entire performance.' By the end of that remarkable Saturday Kiri had also managed to track down Desmond and had told him the good news. He had in fact been having lunch with Jean Mallandaine and her parents in Buckinghamshire; Jean recalls that when he got home Des phoned and said, 'She's been on'.

Other New York press notices were equally enthusiastic, with Harriett Johnson in the *New York Post* writing: 'Miss Kanawa, a beautiful brunette, who wore a blond wig on-stage, doesn't look as if she had any Polynesian blood and she has a voice as international as the Met itself. It is a large, full, easily produced soprano that opens up on the top like a luscious rose.' Then the weeklies added their praise, with Leighton Kerner of the *Village Voice* pointing out that although her first successes had been in Mozart, 'She is absolutely splendid in Verdi, judging by last Saturday's Desdemona, and her Maria/Amelia in *Simone Boccanegra*, which I heard in London last October.' He went on to say that her acting in the last scene 'far surpassed, in sheer power to wring the audience's emotions, that of any other Desdemona I have ever seen, either in Shakespeare or Verdi'. The *New Yorker*'s guest critic Desmond Shawe-Taylor described how Teresa Stratas had cancelled three hours before the performance and continued: 'Fortunately the New Zealand soprano, Kiri Te Kanawa, who was to have made her Metropolitan debut in the same role a month later, was already on hand, and stepped bravely into the gap. Her success was something more, I believe, than the customary acclaim for modest talent coupled with pluck; it was the spontaneous recognition of an outstandingly beautiful and graceful lyric soprano with a pure, well-trained voice that she uses like an artist.'

Perhaps best of all was a lengthy article in *New York Magazine* in which Alan Rich discussed in detail finance and politics at the Metropolitan, and wrote: 'The question under all this is, of course, whether the Met is worth saving withal, and all it took was the season's first *Otello* to convince me that it sure withal is. An afternoon like that, with sublime artistry exerted in the service of as great an opera as I know, renders inoperative every negative comment that has come this way.' Having praised Jon Vickers, James Levine, and Fabrizio Melano and his stage crew, Rich concluded: 'It was, most of all, the day of Kiri Te Kanawa, the young New Zealand soprano who took on the Desdemona on two [*sic*] hours' notice. This is a singer with a voice as beautiful as any I have heard in the house since the time of the young Tebaldi – like hers also in its absolute lyric creaminess from top to bottom. Beyond this, hers was not merely an understudy's job of holding a show together; she moved through the opera with regality, utter grace and believability, and the power to wring the heart. Do not miss this glorious artist – in this season's remaining *Otellos*, next season's *Don Giovanni*, or any time she comes your way.'

For Kiri herself, more satisfying than any of these magnificent notices must have been the letter that arrived from John Tooley at Covent Garden the following week and which read: 'Dear Kiri, I was thrilled to hear of your enormous success at the Metropolitan and I send you my warmest congratulations. You have clearly done yourself and everybody proud, and that makes me very happy . . . We look forward to having you back with us again soon. With my best wishes, Yours sincerely, John Tooley.' She had proved her point, and in the pleasantest and happiest way possible.

The New York reviews were followed by a spate of feature articles and interviews by journalists eager to make themselves and their readers better acquainted with the attractive soprano who seemed likely to be a big name around New York for years to come. Kiri recalls: 'I seemed to end up by giving about six interviews a day, and I found the constant talking and saying the same thing over and over again very boring. It was funny really because when I went to New York, Basil had said I should have a press agent as I was making my debut well on into the run and might not get noticed otherwise. So I got one – but by the "official" first night all the agent had to do was to sit back and make the dates.'

During that four-week wait Kiri's supporters began to arrive in New York. First Desmond and Jean Mallandaine, who came a week early to prepare a recital she and Kiri were due to give and found Kiri was 'snowed under with press interviews with the telephone ringing non-stop'. Then Vera and Basil Horsfield arrived, so the official debut on 7 March took place with her husband, teacher, managers and friends in the audience, and drew a fifteen-minute ovation at the final curtain which prompted Kiri to comment afterwards to a journalist: 'Des says I've never had such a reception at Covent Garden. I'm pleased and my singing teacher, Vera Rozsa, was so proud. I could feel the warmth coming through from the audience and this helped me a lot. I think it went a lot better than on my first appearance here.' The performance took place the day after her thirtieth birthday, and the day before it the City of New York had given her a birthday present in the form of their civic scroll. It was presented by the Deputy Mayor, James Cavanagh, on behalf of the Mayor, Abe Beame. The citation was for 'disttinguished and exceptional service' and continued: 'Her contribution to the art of opera is of inestimable value.' The award drew the following cable from New Zealand's Prime Minister, Norman Kirk: 'I have just learned of the honour bestowed on you by the City of New York on Tuesday by the presentation of a civic scroll, a richly deserved tribute from a city of great discernment in operatic art. I congratulate you on behalf of all New Zealanders. I hope you have a relaxed and enjoyable birthday, and I know that in your formal debut at the Metropolitan you will enhance an already fine reputation. With best wishes.'

There remained three more performances to sing at the Met and one other engagement just outside New York, at Great Neck on Long Island, where Sam Niefeld had arranged a recital for her, accompanied by Jean Mallandaine. She sang a well-balanced programme of Bellini, Rossini, a group of Richard Strauss songs, the Countess's two arias from *Figaro*, Dvorak's 'Gypsy Songs' – still in her repertoire from those early New Zealand days – and, of course, Desdemona's 'Willow Song' and 'Ave Maria' from the final scene of *Otello*. Between her fourth and final performances of *Otello* in New York Kiri had to fly back to England to fit in two performances of Beethoven's Choral Symphony with the London Philharmonic Orchestra conducted by Bernard Haitink. This meant leaving New York on 26 March, rehearsing the concert on the 28th, with performances at the Fairfield Hall, Croydon on the 30th and at the Festival Hall on the 31st. After that she had a few days at home in Esher before flying back to New York on 9 April in time for her final performance at the Met on 13 April.

Well though they went, and enthusiastically as they were received, Kiri's performances as Desdemona in Covent Garden's revival of *Otello* during May were, inevitably, something of an anti-climax for her. The excited anticipation, nervous tension and ultimate triumph had already happened in New York: in London it was a question of performing the role in Covent Garden's over

[135]

twenty-year-old production to the best of her ability and well enough to explain and justify the excitement that had crossed the Atlantic ahead of her. This production remains in the Royal Opera's repertory in Georges Wakhevitch's admittedly evocative and atmospheric but now sadly shabby 1955 designs, and Kiri feels that of all Covent Garden's current productions this is the one that most urgently needs replacing, adding, 'If I had the money, I'd pay for it myself!' Nevertheless the original producer, Peter Potter, had returned to rehearse this 1974 revival, and one of Britain's most distinguished and experienced Verdians, Charles Mackerras, was in the pit to conduct an impressive cast, with Carlo Cossutta as Otello and Piero Cappuccilli as Iago. The revival went well and Kiri sang quite beautifully, moving with considerable assurance around the antiquated sets, and investing the role with the pathos, dignity and, above all, the innocence it so emphatically requires and yet so rarely receives. At the same time there was a slight self-consciousness about her performance: it was almost a demonstration of a lesson that had been superbly learned in New York and was now being reproduced on Covent Garden's stage. One could begin to understand why the Royal Opera's management had been so keen that she should perform Desdemona for the first time in London: the challenge of the first attempt at a role so often seems to bring out the very best of Kiri's qualities, above all, her marvellous spontaneity.

She received a thoroughly enthusiastic and approving set of notices in the British press, though Desmond Shawe-Taylor who, unlike most of his London colleagues, had seen her in New York, did observe that she was not quite so radiant and tender of tone as at the Metropolitan, but continued: 'She gave us nevertheless as lovely a Desdemona as most of us can recall; it is a role to which she is ideally suited, alike in looks and voice.' Even Martin Cooper, not hitherto an apparent admirer of her work, noted in the *Daily Telegraph* that she made 'a touching and dignified Desdemona' and gave the 'Ave Maria' 'an almost child-like purity of tone achieved with a faultless technical command'. In *The Times* William Mann was almost totally carried away, writing, 'Desdemonas are expected to interpret the "Willow Song" and "Ave Maria", and the third act duet and finale, and the end of the choral serenade, and numerous great moments in the first act love duet, with all the angelic qualities that Miss Te Kanawa brings to them. They usually don't, and hopeful Desdemonas must sense the green-eyed monster of jealousy when they hear her mould these and other famous passages so effortlessly and beautifully, looking all the while so perfectly in character and so sumptuously edible.' Harold Rosenthal likewise claimed in *Opera* that her Desdemona was 'one of the finest heard at Covent Garden since Renata Tebaldi in 1950' and continued: 'Her acting has improved out of all recognition and her commitment to the role was complete.' With notices at that level, Kiri had little reason to feel displeased with her performance.

At the beginning of June, hard on the heels of this triumphant *Otello* at the Garden came a rather pallid revival of *Carmen* in the previous year's new production, with Kiri again singing Micaela. Carmen was Tatiana Troyanos (who was the following year to record the role with Kiri as Micaela for Decca, conducted by Georg Solti) and Jean Bonhomme was Don José but it was Kiri's Micaela and José Van Dam's Escamillo who were generally admired in the press, even though Martin Cooper in the *Daily Telegraph* found Kiri 'ill at ease, and her voice not at its best in "Je dis" ' and Philip Hope-Wallace in the *Guardian* observed that, 'Kiri Te Kanawa, much applauded, really made very little of "Je dis que rien ne m'épouvante" with a hustled and squally climax.' But at that point Kiri at Covent Garden, save possibly in the eyes of some of the older and harder-headed music critics, could virtually do no wrong. Christopher Grier, writing in the *Evening Standard*, summed up popular feeling when he wrote: 'The fact that Micaela's Act 3 song stole the show tells you something about last night's revival of Bizet's *Carmen*. Granted the part was played by everybody's operatic sweetheart, Kiri Te Kanawa, with an endearing simplicity quite untainted by sloppiness; more to the point it was splendidly sung.'

From *Carmen* at Covent Garden Kiri moved on to another

series as the Countess in Glyndebourne's production of *The Marriage of Figaro*. A foretaste of her performance had been offered to a far larger audience than Glyndebourne's in May, when Southern Television's film of the production, made the previous year, by David Heather, was networked nationally on commercial television. This year John Pritchard, Kenneth Montgomery and Peter Gellhorn shared the conducting and Kiri had a new Count in the tall, handsome American baritone, Michael Devlin, with whom she got on splendidly. This production of *Figaro* was performed complete, with Pritchard once again conducting, as part of the BBC's 1974 season of Prom concerts at the Royal Albert Hall. Needless to say the hall's over-six-thousand capacity was filled and Kiri responded magnificently, in her Proms debut, to the challenge of projecting the Countess's character and predicament without the assistance of scenery or costumes, drawing such adjectives as 'glorious' and 'moving' from the assembled critics. It was indeed deeply moving and impressive: the arena was packed with Prommers listening in rapt silence punctuated only by gusts of unaffected laughter at the exquisitely managed comedy. In the *Guardian* Philip Hope-Wallace found there had been positive rewards in this Prom form of presentation, writing: 'It is as if the company, at the end of its Sussex Festival, found in the huge circus tent of ten times their home ground an encouragement and a stimulus to project their roles with special vigour. The performance simply fizzed.'

After a short holiday Kiri was back in England during September, and in the early part of the month started work on a BBC Television 'Profile' about her, produced by Patricia Foy for BBC2. In it, Kiri sang a number of her best-loved pieces, including 'Dove sono', 'Mi tradì', Desdemona's 'Willow Song' and, of course, the Maori Farewell. She did not merely sing: she was also interviewed extensively by Bernard Levin, who had been one of her keenest fans from an early stage and to whom she responded quite superbly for the cameras. When the programme appeared in December 1975 the following year a new public saw her, both at home and at work, looking friendly and relaxed – a typically down-to-earth New

Zealand girl, neither starstruck nor snobbish, not talking in terms of 'my career', but of 'my job' and doing it just as well as she was able.

A by-product of this television programme was Kiri's decision to reveal publicly the fact that she had been adopted – something previously only known to her immediate circle of family and friends. 'Bernard Levin was one of the people who already knew – as we'd talked about it before. But while Bernard was down at Esher with Paddy Foy and the rest of the BBC team, Daddy was also staying with me and I explained to him how difficult it would be to explain to the television people that I had a half-sister and so on, and that eventually I'd have to come clean. I thought this would be the perfect opportunity to say I was adopted at a very young age and that my mother had been married twice, so that from then on they'd stop asking me all these difficult questions. I had to ask Daddy's permission and if he'd said "no" I wouldn't have done it.' Kiri's love and respect for her father have always been paramount. In her early life in New Zealand she felt he had treated her as a real, everyday person, something far more important to both of them than merely being gifted with a voice. It was Tom who had taught her how to fish and how to play golf, treating her almost as the son he had always wanted and taking her away on weekend trips in his truck. Kiri also inherited from him her desire for privacy: whilst Nell liked nothing better than to have the press in daily attendance at their Auckland home to describe, report and photograph her daughter's latest achievements, Tom would slip away and continue quietly with his own life, perfectly happy to remain in the background until he was truly needed. So it is with Kiri today: she accepts, even welcomes, press attention as a necessary ingredient of her work, but her home life with her family is kept quite separate – it is truly her private life.

At the end of September Kiri left for a week's holiday with Desmond's family in Brisbane, after which she moved on to Sydney for a series of five concerts with the New Zealand Broadcasting Corporation Orchestra conducted by Brian Priestman. She sang three times in Sydney – twice in the Opera House, the other concert in the town hall – and gave a concert apiece in Canberra and Adelaide. She performed the same work at each concert – the *Four Last Songs* of Richard Strauss – and received highly enthusiastic coverage from the Australian press. This included a feature in the *Sydney Sunday Telegraph* by Maria Prerauer, who remembered hearing Kiri sing in the *Sydney Sun* aria contest a decade earlier which she had failed to win. It was headlined: 'Kiri takes her revenge in full', and described her visit as a 'just retribution for the Sydney judges, and for the eisteddfodau cult'. Ms Prerauer considered that Kiri had now returned in triumph and that 'Her voice, especially the incredibly beautiful top, sounded absolutely radiant. It has an unmistakable timbre, a wonderfully personal characteristic quality that almost defies definition. Here is warmth with controlled power, creaminess with sensuousness, flexibility with spaciousness. And it is backed by supreme intelligence, and an emotional artist's temperament.'

Although Kiri was singing with a New Zealand orchestra she didn't cross the Tasman Sea to sing in her homeland, and New Zealanders had to content themselves with a television recording of one of her concerts, shown by NZBC throughout the country the following month. They had, however, been told that thanks to sponsorship by Benson and Hedges Kiri would be singing in New Zealand again in August of the following year. New Zealanders accepted that prior commitments prevented her from singing there as well as in Australia in 1974 – indeed rehearsals for Covent Garden's new production of *Faust*, in which she was singing Marguerite, began within days of her return to London from Australia – but a feeling of disquiet was growing that their beloved home-grown soprano was becoming too famous and too busy to sing in her native land. The *Auckland Star* did indeed point out that these would be her first public engagements in New Zealand since 1972, but Juan Matteucci, the conductor of the Symphonia of Auckland with whom Kiri would be singing in 1975, was quoted: 'It's marvellous to have a fantastic artist of such calibre appearing with the orchestra. There's no doubt that Kiri is now a major international star and it will be great to have her back.'

The next phase of Kiri's life turned out to be an altogether less happy one. The five years of sustained and unremitting hard work and high pressure since she first joined Covent Garden in 1970 caused a serious breakdown in her normally robust health. The Royal Opera's new production of Gounod's *Faust*, the first since 1938, was the starting point of her troubles. John Davern, Basil Horsfield's partner as Kiri's manager, describes it now as 'the operatic equivalent of Macbeth: an ill-starred production in which everything that could go wrong, did'. The first problem for Kiri was that Desmond had stayed on in Western Australia to work for at least the next six months on an engineering project near Perth. This meant she was entirely alone, except for her Siamese cat, Cobber, at the house in Esher and had to drive every day from there to the still-dreaded London Opera Centre for rehearsals before returning, exhausted, to an empty house each evening.

Norman Treigle, the American bass who was star of the New York City Opera and who was making his Covent Garden debut as Mephistopheles, failed to arrive in time for the start of rehearsals, and when he did eventually arrive, he promptly damaged his foot, and thus missed rehearsals anyway. In addition the conductor, John Matheson, started missing rehearsals too, because he was busy correcting Gounod's score and opening the traditional cuts, which in itself gave Kiri a lot of new music to learn at very short notice. She says now, '*Faust* was an awful time: I was terribly unhappy, Des was away and rehearsals at the Opera Centre seemed to be going on for weeks and weeks.'

Moreover, although John Copley was producing *Faust* and he and Kiri could be seen having their usual high-spirited time during rehearsals on an Aquarius television programme shown shortly before the first night, the role of Marguerite never really engaged Kiri's attention and affection in the way that her favourite Mozart and Verdi roles had done. When the first night finally arrived on 22 November, Kiri gave a sound and thoroughly competent performance; but, by her own high standards, she seemed less than totally involved and her voice, though true, never really caught fire, not even in the famous 'Jewel Song' which had been in her repertoire since New Zealand days. That first night was a Friday and after it Kiri spent a dismal weekend, knowing that neither the production nor her performance had been an out-an-out success. Basil Horsfield and John Davern gave a party for her and the rest of the cast on the Saturday night, but she was far from her normal ebulliently cheerful self, instead looking very young, very lost and totally forlorn. John Davern remembers, 'She was so lonely she stayed the night with us instead of going back to Esher. On the Sunday we all went to see the film *Murder on the Orient Express* and Kiri fell asleep in the cinema!'

Kiri recognizes that she was under-powered in *Faust*: 'I don't think I was that bad, but I just didn't seem to have the energy to push it out. Vera said it was one of those things I just had to pay for and that it was even good when something goes wrong like that, as it brings me back to earth.' The reviews were in fact respectful, if not wholly enthusiastic. Ronald Crichton in the *Financial Times* commented that the 'girlish timbre' of her Marguerite was overdone and that in the prison scene she was 'unable or unwilling to sing out in the all-or-nothing final trio'. Peter Heyworth in the *Observer* considered that, 'As Marguerite, Kiri Te Kanawa has the necessary reserves of power, and she sings touchingly in the love music. But the middle register of her soft-grained voice frequently fails to penetrate the orchestra, and her account of the "Jewel Song" explains why the French like to mix a little metal into the tone of their sopranos.' William Mann in *The Times*, however, was as loyal as always and considered that she made 'a radiant and touching Marguerite'. Still, there was no gainsaying the fact that notices such as these were not what Kiri had become accustomed to in recent years, and they did little to cheer her up.

She was at least amongst friends in the cast. Stuart Burrows was singing Faust and Anne Howells was Siebel. She recalls, 'Kiri was depressed about her reviews for *Faust*, which truly hadn't gone well, and Des was away. So I went round to her place one evening and had a curry with her, and she asked me to stay the night. She

brought me television in the bath and glasses of wine, but I had to
ask her to have the place a little cooler: it was like Rangoon in the
rainy season, so hot I could see the plants opening! Then she couldn't
get to sleep and just as I was dropping off she suddenly snapped on
the light and started plucking her eyebrows. It was clearly not a
happy time for her.' Nor, as it turned out, was it a happy time for
Anne Howells. She had had a cartilage problem for a long time and
one night later in the run, while she was singing, her cartilage went
out and she was thrown across the stage. 'The curtain came down
instantly,' says Anne, 'as I just couldn't sing. Kiri was in her dressing-
room, heard the sudden silence and thought, "It's got to be Annie's
knee." She came rushing out to find me lying there moaning, so
Marguerite, Faust and Mephistopheles had to carry me off to my
dressing-room.'

The final disaster hit the production when John Matheson, who
had seemed unhappy as conductor from the outset, finally withdrew
because of ill health after the fourth performance, and Charles
Mackerras was brought in to replace him at twenty-four hours'
notice. This happened on the day Kiri was at home filming the final
sequences of her interview with Bernard Levin for Patricia Foy's
television profile. The tug of war that developed between the Royal
Opera House and the BBC as to who had first claim on Kiri's
services and where she should spend the remainder of the day may
have made for one of Levin's wittiest articles in *The Times* the following week, but did little to improve Kiri's equanimity at the time.

Luckily, after the final performance of *Faust* in the middle of
December (and to date it has proved literally to be her final performance as Marguerite) she could look forward in the new year to
returning to a role she knew and loved – Donna Elvira in Mozart's
Don Giovanni. She was to sing two series of the opera, the first in New
York at the Metropolitan Opera during January, and the second in a
new production which would mark her debut at the Paris Opéra
during February and March.

The Met performances were in a straightforward revival of an
existing production, indeed the opera had already been performed

there before Christmas, and Kiri was merely one of a number of cast changes. Nevertheless, her appearance made its usual mark and attracted the usual warm reception in the press, with William Zakariasen in the *New York Daily News* writing: 'The big news was the first appearance of the stunning young soprano from New Zealand, Kiri Te Kanawa, in the pivotal role of Donna Elvira. "Donna Elektra" almost would seem a better name, for upon [her] first entrance, eyes glaring, chestnut hair tousled and her pace like that of a caged tigress, it was plain that this was no standard shrinking violet impersonation.' He went on to say, 'She is also a singer whose attractive voice is more than large enough for the role, and whose technique and musicianship are next to flawless. Applause for her second-act aria "Mi tradì" was volcanic; no wonder – a better rendition of it today seems inconceivable.'

Jean Mallandaine was with Kiri in New York, for at the end of the *Don Giovanni* run she was to accompany her in a broadcast recital to be given at the house of the beautiful Frick Collection off Fifth Avenue. Before that, just after the first night, there had been a large reception given in Kiri's honour by the British Consul-General in New York. Kiri has amused memories of that particular evening. 'There were about two hundred people there, of whom I knew hardly anyone. One Canadian lady came up to me and told me she didn't know who I was or why I was there, so I told her I was New Zealand's answer to Joan Sutherland!' The recital at the Frick Collection was a more serious occasion; the programme consisted of Handel, Purcell (Dido's 'Lament', which she had not sung since leaving the Opera Centre), Schumann, a group of Richard Strauss songs and a group by British composers, including her original party piece 'Do not go, my love'. It went extremely well.

The New York trip ended with a broadcast matinée performance of *Don Giovanni* on 1 February, and after that Kiri flew to Paris to start rehearsals of the Paris Opéra's new production of the same work. This would be the first time *Don Giovanni* had been seen at the Opéra since 1964; it would be produced by August Everding, with designs by Toni Businger and to Kiri's joy would be conducted by Georg Solti. For Kiri, the result was a profound love affair with Paris, fully reciprocated. Although Everding's production and Roger Soyer's Don Giovanni – he had in fact sung the role with her the previous month in New York – were not universally liked, the French papers vied with one another for superlatives in describing Kiri's performance.

Le Figaro identified her as 'The queen of the evening', and went on to advise its readers that 'This ravishing creature possesses a voice of incomparable suppleness and mellowness . . . the timbre of one's dreams for Mozart.' In L'Aurore Pierre Julien wrote about 'the beautiful, seductive, astonishing New Zealander, Kiri Te Kanawa, with us for the first time. Her Donna Elvira . . . would be enough reason in itself to go to the Palais Garnier. One has rarely seen on stage a singer who deployed such physical and vocal seductive-ness . . . Here was the Elvira for whom we have been waiting a long time.' In the Quotidien de Paris Gerard Mannoni was reminded of Elisabeth Schwarzkopf. Kiri struck gold in the English press as well, with Alan Blyth praising her in The Times for 'singing as flawless as it was impassioned', and pointing out that 'both donne benefited from Solti's marvellous realization of orchestral detail in their arias' – for Solti, along with Margaret Price and José Van Dam as Leporello, were the other heroes of the production. Finally, in the May issue of Opera, Charles Pitt wrote a perceptive account of her performance. 'It was the ladies that stole the show. Margaret Price's Donna Anna was as glorious as ever, and Kiri Te Kanawa made a highly successful Paris debut as Elvira, and made one regret the fact that she recorded the role too soon. Beautiful, passionate, and accurate and powerful at both limits of her range – lower D to upper B – how could Giovanni have ever deserted her? Te Kanawa's terrifying obsessiveness gives the answer. She alone loves Giovanni through thick and thin, and in this production she is always careful never to ally herself fully with the avenging Anna and Ottavio.'

Sadly, despite her colossal success in Paris, which included a visit to the performance by the then French President, Valéry Giscard d'Estaing, Kiri was unable fully to enjoy the time she spent there. She had not been well in New York – in fact she had suffered an early miscarriage during the run of *Don Giovanni*. 'I realized only afterwards that that was what it had been. I was a few months pregnant and knew I didn't feel very well, but being me, I didn't miss any performances – just hung on in there!' The lifestyle in Paris over-burdened her already weakened constitution. 'It was my first time there and it all proved too much: living alone in an hotel with Des still being away, the after-effects of the miscarriage in New York, so much rich food, plus all the rushing around – I just couldn't take it. The result was a recurrence of my hepatitis, but this time far worse than before.' Kiri had been attending a doctor in Paris since the middle of February who found that her condition had deteriorated whilst she was there, and when she returned to London at the end of March she was feeling far from well.

Upon her return Kiri was supposed to be working on two new roles: first Mimi in *La Bohème* with Scottish Opera in May, and then her first Fiordiligi in Mozart's *Così fan tutte* at Covent Garden during June and July. But her regular doctor in London, Dr Briggs, having seen her in the middle of March, reported that she still had abnormalities of liver function and was also suffering from 'anxiety-depression'; he strongly advised her to rest completely for at least three months. The result was Covent Garden's announcement on her behalf at the end of March: 'Miss Kiri Te Kanawa is suffering from anxiety depression aggravated by symptoms of abnormal liver function which became evident while rehearsing in Paris earlier this month. After medical advice there and from her London advisers, it has reluctantly been decided that the only course open is for her to cancel all engagements for April, May and June so that a complete cure can be effected.' Scottish Opera were not happy and neither were London audiences who had been much looking forward to Kiri's first Fiordiligi; but if she were to continue singing at all, the break was essential. Kiri was particularly grateful to Sir John Tooley at Covent Garden, whose considerable help and understanding made things much easier for her.

It was vital that Kiri's whereabouts during the next three months should be unknown by the press or anyone else. In fact, she went to Perth in Western Australia, where Desmond was working, for what was in effect a second honeymoon. 'It was wonderful, and gave Des and me another chance to get to know each other – we'd been apart so much in the past few years. Perth is one of the most beautiful cities in the world; once I got there I was almost immediately back on form mentally, but I had to get my body back on form too. It was a lovely period: Des and I lived in a self-contained apartment in a motel, and after two weeks of doing nothing at all I slowly got back to work. Des found someone to play the piano for me, and I learned all the music I had to learn. I relearned *Boccanegra*, and studied Pamina in *The Magic Flute*, then *Così* and *Bohème*. After we'd both finished work for the day we'd play lots of golf, and I'd have dinner ready for Des. I was about twenty pounds overweight when all this happened, so Des went on a diet with me to help me. We had enormous fun and I met all his friends out there. I never thought of quitting: it was just one of those things that happened in my life, and now I was recuperating.'

For Desmond, Kiri's major illness and subsequent convalescence led to a more far-reaching decision. 'My going away to Australia had caused problems. I suppose when we first got married and I went single-status to Iran for an extended period it was OK, but with every year Kiri was depending more on me. I had to stay on in Perth if I wanted to make my mark and get on, but it wasn't working out for the two of us – so I pulled out. I realized that immersing myself in work twenty-four hours a day, seven days a week wasn't any good, and that if I continued, the same thing would happen to Kiri again. So I turfed that life in, left the company I'd been working for more or less since we were married, and went into business on my own. It's much better – I can adjust my schedule to fit Kiri's and give her support when she needs it.'

None of this had occurred because of any fundamental physical weakness in Kiri: far from it. She has a strong constitution and is always at pains to keep herself fit, with plenty of exercise, and to maintain her ideal singing weight of just over eleven stone. She drinks sparingly – wine and never spirits – and doesn't smoke – in fact she abhors the habit and is forever trying to persuade Desmond and her friends to give it up. She eats healthily, preferring her own simple but excellent cooking at home, with plenty of salads, to richer food in restaurants. Moreover she has a reputation in her profession for virtually never cancelling a performance, and even for dissuading opera-house managements from craving the audience's indulgence on her behalf when she is suffering from a cold or sore throat. Nevertheless the strains of constant performances and recording sessions, tense, sometimes fraught, rehearsal periods, air travel and consequent jet-lag, living alone in hotels or apartments in foreign cities are considerable. Up to 1976 Kiri had been attempting to do too much on her own, and she and Desmond had been leading over-separate lives. Since then they have become much more of a unit and their family life has become even closer since the arrival of their two children. Today, however serious a temporary professional set-back she may suffer, there is always her home and her family to return to for support and reassurance.

II

—◦•◦—

Six New Roles and Motherhood

KIRI'S ILLNESS IN 1975 was a watershed in her life. From that point on she and Desmond faced life together, albeit with regular but relatively short separations as they went about their respective jobs. From then on, too, she no longer tackled more than one new role at the same time, as she had regularly done since joining Covent Garden five years earlier. As she puts it, 'My illness wasn't a catastrophe, but everybody realized after it that they couldn't push me too far. Not that it had been Basil's, or Covent Garden's or anybody else's fault. I'd had nothing but good advice up to then, but from then on everybody has tended to watch me, and to see to it that I didn't overdo things. I'd crammed too much in – it had been my own fault for saying yes. The trouble basically is that my voice is very soft-grained, and will only take a certain amount of work: above all it can't stand tackling one opera in conjunction with another. It's a bit like a Ferrari, if it's not kept properly tuned, it's not going to go. If I had a voice like an old Mini that can stand out in the cold and rain and start first time, then I could probably tackle a far greater number of roles; but it's not – and I can't!' She had also, by her return from Australia in 1975, evolved a complete system of learning new roles, to which she still adheres. 'It starts with me on my own. A pianist like Jean Mallandaine or, now that she's mostly in America, probably Peter Robinson or John Bacon, will put the

[149]

role on tape for me, just my own vocal line plus the entrances and exits of other parts, with piano accompaniment. I'll listen to that a lot because I'm still not a good sight reader and the tape's my best way of getting to know the part and the music. Then, once I've broken the back of it, I'll start going to a pianist to coach me. As well as the music I'll learn the words, read them through many times and mark everything out. I can read French and Italian easily, but German is still a bit difficult. After that I'll go, with the pianist, to Vera, and by the time I get to her I'll already know the part. I'll also get some recordings of the opera I'm studying, three or four different sets if possible, but I won't listen to them before I've broken the back of the part. Then I'll set aside one whole day for listening to the recordings. I get so many because that way they'll get fuddled together in my mind and I won't have any one singer's interpretation in my head. For example, with *La Traviata* I only really listened to Callas's recording after my performances because her singing is so wonderful and it would be terrible subconsciously to ape it. I think I can honestly say I've never aped another singer's performance, because I've always wanted to be me.

'Another thing I might well do is to go and see the opera. With *Arabella*, for example, I flew specially to Cologne to see it, because I'd never seen it before or even read the story. I wanted to see it first through the eyes of someone who didn't understand it at all. Then all the next day I read through the words and listened to the tape, and it fell into place. So, when I'm ready, I go to Vera, and she teaches me about the role's technical problems and how to last out the opera, as well as a lot of interpretation. It's the lasting out that's vital: to go from the beginning to the end of the opera, and to come out saying I could do that all over again. The New York Met's marvellous conductor, Jimmy Levine, for example, insists on that. I remember once in New York at the end of a *Figaro*, where I'd sung the Countess and he listened in the wings, he went and sat down at the piano, with me still in my costume, and made me sing Fiordiligi's two big arias, "Come scoglio" and "Per pietà" – just to prove that my voice was still fresh!

[150]

'With Vera the most important thing first is to get the technical problems over and done with, for example how to breathe a certain phrase. In the first act of *Arabella*, for instance, if you're not careful you can easily sing yourself out for the rest of the opera, so it's important to learn how to relax. The set-up at Vera's is that first I'll do thirty minutes of exercises, then one and a half hours on the music, or the arias. I call it the tops and tails; some people call it the ins and outs – the entrances and exits – but not so much the central sections. There are also all the little knick-knack *parlando* bits which are much harder to sing than a good long phrase. After that, when you get to the rehearsal stage, it's the conductor of course who has the final say on how the tempi should go. If you want to hold up in a certain area and the conductor wants you to go on, then you have to work your own interpretation in. If you tell the conductor you want to do it your way and he says "No, you'll have to change gear," then you can still do it your way, but within his timing!'

Once performances of an opera are under way, however, it is not the conductor upon whom she relies, but the prompter, in his little subterranean box at the front of the stage, facing the singers. 'I depend on the prompter completely: perhaps that is my major problem now. But even if you know a work very well, you can get lost: I remember once I even made a mistake in the middle of "Mi tradì" in *Don Giovanni*, which I've sung countless times. In *Arabella* at Covent Garden Alastair Dawes got me through with his prompting, because I'd told him there were some places I wasn't sure about, where it seemed to go round and round. I tell the prompter that when I look down at him – or her – I want the words immediately. When I look, it means I'm about to get into trouble. I tend never to take any notice of the conductor during a performance: I know his speeds from rehearsals – and it's his business to carry the whole orchestra and chorus, so he already has far too much on his plate to help you. We were always taught at the Opera Centre that the prompter is there to go to if you are in trouble, and being a good prompter is really quite an art. But he mustn't sing my lines, just speak them. There was one who once did sing them and I had to say to him, "Please don't sing it – I know how to sing, it's the words I need!"'

Kiri's first work after returning from Australia was in July with one of her now favourite conductors, Georg Solti, recording *Carmen* for Decca in the Henry Wood Hall in London. But despite her rest she had picked up a throat virus and was still not singing well. 'But Solti was so marvellous: he said "She can't sing, there's something wrong – so we'll wait." And he fixed up some special extra sessions for me in December, and I did my Micaela arias then. That was Solti being really sweet.' After the *Carmen* recording sessions she made a quick trip to the south of France at the end of the month for a performance of the Verdi *Requiem* at the Aix-en-Provence Festival, and of Handel's *Messiah*, conducted by Charles Mackerras, in the ancient Roman amphitheatre at Orange. Having returned to London, she then left for New Zealand at the beginning of August for the five concerts arranged in 1974 with the Symphonia of Auckland, in Auckland, Wellington and Hamilton.

Predictably, her return to her homeland was greeted with enormous enthusiasm. 'Our beloved Kiri has come home,' trumpeted the New Zealand *Woman's Weekly*, advertising an extensive profile by the distinguished New Zealand television personality and journalist, Max Cryer, with one of the photographs taken by Lord Snowdon on its cover. Kiri gave two different programmes at the concerts: Mozart's 'Exsultate jubilate' and 'Come scoglio' from *Così fan tutte*, plus Amelia's aria 'Come in quest'ora' from *Simone Boccanegra* and 'In quelle trine morbide' from Puccini's *Manon Lescaut* at one series; and 'Dove sono' from *Figaro*, 'Ach, ich fühls' from *The Magic Flute*, the 'Jewel Song' from *Faust* and arias by Bellini and Puccini at the other. She was still suffering from the same throat infection which, unusually, was announced to the audiences before the concerts. The fact that she wasn't singing at her best scarcely diminished the enthusiasm of the notices she received – they carped only at the shorter length of her contribution and, in Auckland, at the lack of stage lighting to show her off in the hall. It is true that she sang fewer pieces than in the days of her early marathons at

Brooklands Bowl, but that was all part of Kiri's new approach – learning to pace herself.

From New Zealand it was back to Paris for three more performances as Elvira in *Don Giovanni*, one of which was televised, and luncheon at the Elysée Palace as a guest of President Giscard d'Estaing, before travelling to San Francisco. There she sang Amelia in *Simone Boccanegra*, and her first Pamina in *The Magic Flute*, in Ruth and Thomas Martin's English translation. The *Boccanegra*, with Ingvar Wixell in the title role, was much praised and critics vied with each other for superlatives to describe her performance. *The Magic Flute*, with the Opera's General Director, Kurt Herbert Adler, conducting, was less warmly received, though Kiri was generally praised for her Pamina. The *Daily Californian*'s critic described her performance as 'the one positive note in the evening', adding: 'She was the most vocally confident and accomplished of any of the leading roles, while her stage presence lent a sorely needed authority to the listless dramatic proceedings.' Against that the *San Francisco Chronicle* observed that Kiri's Pamina was 'a sophisticate in a land of innocents, the opposite of the opera's intent. In a stronger cast it might have been wonderful.' Kiri herself would be the first to agree that she had not yet come to terms with an elusive role. Initially she found the part less stimulating than her other Mozart heroines, saying, '*The Magic Flute* has become something I want to do more as I've got older. When I did it first I thought the whole thing was ridiculous. It didn't help doing it in English, a language which I find extremely difficult to sing.' Today she understands the role far better and is much more at home in it, but even so her performances somehow lack the magic and charisma with which she imbues the Countess, Donna Elvira and Fiordiligi.

Her final engagement of 1975, fixed up at short notice while she was in San Francisco, was to go to Vienna to record the Countess in *The Marriage of Figaro* conducted by the great Mozartean Karl Böhm, with a highly distinguished cast including Dietrich Fischer-Dieskau as the Count, Hermann Prey as Figaro, Mirella Freni as Susanna and a then very young mezzo called Maria Ewing as

[153]

Cherubino. The reason for the recording was a Unitel television film to be directed by Jean-Pierre Ponnelle at Shepperton Studios the following year: in the usual way of such enterprises, the music was recorded first and during the filming itself the singers simply 'marked' their parts. Kiri much enjoyed working with Karl Böhm for the first time. 'I got on very well with him, though he tended to get at young singers who have the least confidence. But it's just a question of having the character and ability to withstand criticism. He kept a firm hold on the tempi – they never lagged – and if he took a slow speed, in the same way as Claudio Abbado sometimes does, then you just had to take a bigger breath. But the great thing about Böhm was that he gave you so much time to breathe, and do the tempi the right way with plenty to spare.'

1976 was a busy, highly successful year in which among other things Kiri sang her first Mimì in *La Bohème* at Covent Garden in January, her first Tatyana in Tchaikovsky's *Eugene Onegin*, also at Covent Garden, in April, followed by her first Fiordiligi in Mozart's *Così fan tutte* at the Paris Opéra in May. She was helped through such a demanding programme by the fact that she had fully prepared the roles of Mimì and Fiordiligi in Australia in 1974 during her recuperation.

On the domestic front an even more significant event took place that year when Kiri and Desmond adopted their first child – a daughter, Antonia, invariably known as Toni. They had been thinking about having children since 1974, by which time Kiri felt she was sufficiently established to take time off to have a family. But pregnancy had proved difficult – she had suffered the miscarriage while singing in New York – and of course her own and Desmond's schedules kept them so much apart. As Desmond explains: 'I'm pretty sure that it was originally my suggestion to adopt. But it wasn't something we sat around discussing at great length, just that the suggestion came up and we both thought what a good idea it was. There was certainly no difference for us between having our own child and adopting one.'

Once Toni arrived she was swiftly absorbed into the Park

household, helped by a New Zealand Karitane nannie, Lynne, who remained with them for the next three years. Toni was followed in 1979 by an adopted brother, Thomas, though in the spring of 1977 Kiri had become pregnant again in Paris, and had suffered another miscarriage. In fact this left her, on balance, relieved. 'I was desperately worried about having my own child after Toni. We already loved her so much that it would have been terribly difficult to have had one child who was adopted and then another who was not. We're now a blissfully happy family – the ideal number of children, one of each sex, and both absolutely gorgeous.'

Her first new role of the year, Mimì in Puccini's *La Bohème*, was in John Copley's production which had been new at Covent Garden two years earlier, with Katia Ricciarelli and Placido Domingo in the leading roles. This time the revival was rehearsed by Richard Gregson, one of the Royal Opera's staff producers, and was conducted by the Royal Opera's Chorus Master, the extremely competent Robin Stapleton. Kiri's Rudolfo was Luciano Pavarotti – the first and so far the only time she has sung with this renowned tenor – but apart from him it was virtually a home-grown cast, with Thomas Allen, Richard Van Allan and Stuart Harling as the other Bohemians; Maria Pellegrini, who sang Musetta, though born in Italy, had studied in Canada and had been a member of the Royal Opera in the late 1960s.

Kiri found the rehearsal period went very well, 'Though Pavarotti didn't actually turn up until the dress rehearsal. But he knew it backwards and did it superbly! The first night went marvellously – the audience was buzzing and I felt very good. To have someone of Luciano's quality with you does bring your own standard up.' She received a good press, though the consensus of critical opinion was that she did not really come into her own until the last two acts by which time, Philip Hope-Wallace wrote in the *Guardian*, 'she had the house in tears'. In *The Times* John Higgins wrote: 'To begin with, all the quality was in the voice rather than the figure. "Mi chiamano Mimì" was as musically right as the prim and too correctly dressed appearance was wrong.' Perhaps Christopher

Grier summed it up best when he wrote in the *Evening Standard*: 'Kiri Te Kanawa's Mimì has a problem. She can't help it, but despite her ashen face everything about her proclaims a princess rather than a pretty little tubercular seamstress on her uppers. Such style and beauty would not, I fancy, have been allowed to languish in the Quartier Latin.' The basic difficulty for Kiri in portraying such a character as Mimì (and this applied equally to her Tatyana in *Eugene Onegin* three months later) is that she naturally exudes such an aura of healthy beauty and poised assurance. To portray the fragile Mimì one of life's failures, or the introspective Tatyana, totally lacking in self-confidence, is extremely difficult for her, however well she knows and understands the roles. It is a curious kind of handicap.

Between Mimì and Tatyana came performances of the Countess in Gunther Rennert's production of *Figaro* at the New York Met, which had been new earlier in the season. Kiri found it the worst production of *Figaro* she had ever seen – and boring. This didn't prevent the *New York Post* from headlining her performance: 'Kiri Te Kanawa: a Countess of Beauty, a Joy Forever,' and comparing the sound of her voice with 'the sight of an opalescent pearl', with other critics concurring. Back at Covent Garden in April came the more taxing matter of the revival of Tchaikovsky's *Eugene Onegin*, which had first been seen there in a production by Peter Hall with Solti conducting in 1971. Sadly, Hall had nothing to do with this revival which was in the hands of one of the Royal Opera's staff producers, Charles Hamilton, who seemed unable to extract the best from Kiri. The cast had Benjamin Luxon as Onegin, Stuart Burrows singing Lensky and two fellow New Zealanders, Heather Begg and Patricia Payne, as Tatyana's mother Larina and Nurse Filipyevna. The opera was sung in David Lloyd-Jones's English translation, and was conducted by a young Polish newcomer to Covent Garden, Kazimierz Kord, who has not reappeared there.

Shortly before the opening night on 26 April Kiri gave an interview to Alan Blyth for *The Times*. She admitted she was a slow learner and said she had taken a year to study Tatyana, continuing: 'I was frightened of this one, the depth of it. You can't really experience a role until you're up there singing it. I find it hard, in any case, to play an introverted character since I'm not made that way myself. With Tatyana there's the additional problem of the apparent change in her character between the beginning and the end. I think you have to suggest in the young, ingenuous girl the inner strength of purpose that enables her to act as she does in the last scene. By then she and Onegin are equals, but the spark of determination must come forth and does so in the letter-writing scene. No girl in her right mind in those days could have done such a thing without real spirit. It helps to establish a continuity if, as we have done, you go back and forth between what I call the berry-picking scene and the last scene; then the opposites come together.' She says now, 'I've seen Ileana Cotrubas do it and, especially in the Letter aria, I feel I hadn't got that innocence that Ileana portrays. I think better direction might have helped me and I would much preferred to have sung it in Russian, but it would have taken me three months to learn to sing phonetically. I haven't sung Tatyana since: but I think I could do the letter scene better now, because I know more.'

The first night was nevertheless rapturously received by the audience, who pelted her with flowers at her final curtain, and it was warmly reviewed by the critics, though their notices generally recorded that while she had sung superbly, she had failed to dramatize the role with total conviction. Kiri herself, for once reacting, was convinced that at least some of the critics must have seen her performance at the dress rehearsal and the deficiencies in that. 'From what I could assess, it was what I had done in the dress rehearsal that was commented on but that was totally different from my first performance. Vera told me all the things I'd done wrong at the dress rehearsal, and I'd done my best to put them right.' Vera herself says of that performance: 'She needs a producer who gives her the reasons why she should do what he wants her to do. She won't act if she doesn't know why she should do it. Many times after a dress rehearsal we have vocal and other discussions. After *Onegin*'s I took courage and said, "Kiri, this is boring." She agreed but said, "I don't know why I should do this and that." The producer thought she had no idea, but it was because he hadn't explained to her how and why the character behaves. If Kiri knows the character, and the character is someone she understands, she's fine. In fact she has a tremendous temperament, but she can be very cool if she's not inspired. If she is inspired, then she can be better in a role than anyone else.'

A role by which she was altogether more inspired was her next, Fiordiligi in Mozart's *Così fan tutte*, which she sang for the first time in Paris the following month, and again at Covent Garden in November. Kiri finds the character of Fiordiligi, the elder, more pensive and serious sister 'very demanding and very fulfilling. With Elvira in *Don Giovanni* you're absolutely your own boss, whereas in *Così* Fiordiligi has to work closely with all the other characters. Both roles attract me equally, and the sheer vocal beauty of *Così* is so marvellous. I think Fiordiligi really does fall in love with Ferrando in the second act, because she's more thoughtful, less flighty than her sister Dorabella. She takes longer to make up her mind, but once she's done so she means it.'

The Paris performances in Jean-Pierre Ponnelle's recent production went very well and, in Kiri's words, 'The reviews were all raves – you just have to sing well in Paris and they'll forgive you anything!' One attractive by-product of these Paris performances was the advertisement she made for Rolex watches. Headlined 'For a pearl among opera singers, an oyster' it has regularly appeared in magazines throughout the world since the end of 1976, and shows her in Ponnelle's marvellous costume, a creamy silk and lace dress, with exquisite broad-brimmed 'picture' hat, standing on the main staircase of the Opéra. It unquestionably makes a very pretty picture.

During the summer, between her two visits to Paris, the second for another Fiordiligi and for Elvira in the Opéra's Mozart Festival, Kiri also filmed the Countess in Ponnelle's television production of *Figaro* at Shepperton Studios. She found this immensely enjoyable, despite having to fit it in amongst performances in Paris, and the strain of filming during the hottest part of a very hot summer. The film was not in fact shown on British television, by the BBC, until

March 1981, nearly five years after it was made, such are the vagaries of televison programming.

After the Paris Mozart Festival Kiri briefly visited her father at his house on Lake Taupo in New Zealand en route for Australia to sing first Amelia in *Boccanegra* and then Mimì at the Sydney Opera House. On this visit she fell foul of the local press, whom she resented for not having done their homework and thus asking pointless and unnecessary questions. This resulted in such Australian headlines as 'Beautiful voice, tart tongue,' and, worse, 'Who's bad, bitchy, and beautiful?', as well as comments about her 'killer instinct' and 'solid right jab'. Her performances were nevertheless well received, her Amelia more so than her Mimì, whom the *Sydney Morning Herald*'s critic found 'one of the least moving or affecting in recent memory'. Audiences, however, lapped up her performances – in New Zealand travel agents were offering package tours by air across the Tasman to hear her sing in Sydney.

Back in London Kiri gave a special concert at Covent Garden in aid of United World Colleges and the New Zealand Scholarship Fund, under the Presidency of Earl Mountbatten of Burma and in the presence of Prince Michael of Kent, with the Royal Opera House Orchestra conducted by Kenneth Montgomery. She sang seven arias in all, including 'Porgi amor', 'Per pietà', the 'Jewel Song' from *Faust*, 'Come in quest'ora bruna' from *Boccanegra*, and finally 'Mi chiamano Mimì'. There was a party at the New Zealand High Commission in her honour afterwards, and she later received a charming personal letter of thanks from Lord Mountbatten.

The notices for this concert were good, though not nearly good enough for her greatest fan, Bernard Levin, who thundered about them two days later in *The Times*. 'Did you ever read such a pack of miserable, spiritless wretches as the critics who reviewed the performance in yesterday's papers? What thin and vinegary liquor has been substituted for blood in the veins of Mr Hope-Wallace, for instance, that he could say her performance of the 'Jewel Song' "failed to excite"? What ailed our own Mr Higgins, a most learned and sharp-eared canary-fancier, that he found the evening "a shade unsatisfying"? Failed to excite? A shade unsatisfying? I tell you, if this pair had been present at the miracle of the loaves and fishes, one of them would have complained that there was no lemon to go with the fish, and the other would have demanded more butter for the bread. It was left to Miss Elizabeth Forbes in the *Financial Times* to save the reviewers' honour by communicating something of the concert's pleasure.' In the rest of a lengthy, but highly enjoyable article, Levin analysed Kiri's quality and explained why he considered her 'among the three of four outstanding singers in the world and, to my ear, the possessor of the loveliest voice of them all'.

When it came to Covent Garden's revival of *Così fan tutte* the following month, there was no shortage of critical enthusiasm for her performance. John Copley was there to revive his 1968 production with a home-grown cast – Kiri and Josephine Veasey as the two sisters, Ryland Davies and Thomas Allen as their suitors, Norma Burrowes as Despina and Richard Van Allan as Don Alfonso. Stuart Bedford conducted. In fact it was a very tiring time for Kiri: it came at the end of a busy year, Toni was just settling into the household in Esher and Kiri was having to come to terms with the duties as well as the joys of motherhood, with the problems of 2 a.m. feeds. Despite, or perhaps because of all that, she gave herself unstintingly to the revival and turned in magnificent performances, rapturously received by press and public alike. In the *Evening Standard* Christopher Grier wrote: 'When she took her curtain call last night at the end of *Così fan tutte*, Kiri Te Kanawa was bombarded with flowers from the gallery. She had richly earned them as well as the formal bouquets and the insistent applause. She had just sung Fiordiligi for the first time at Covent Garden. It was a captivating performance of such style, sensitivity, charm and intelligence that one almost wept with pleasure.' How right he was. She had moved around the stage with the grace of total assurance, and had shown great insight into Fiordiligi's character. Maintaining her dignity, reticence and fidelity to the absent Guglielmo during the first act, and then, in the second, powerfully evoking Fiordiligi's gradual, vulnerable and ultimately

[160]

total passion for Ferrando in his Albanian disguise. 'Per pietà' was a moving and disturbing experience, and exquisitely sung. As well as singing like an angel in her two major arias, Kiri also blended superbly into the ensembles of this tightly-knit, wonderfully cohesive opera. It was indeed the performance of a star, but of a star with the utmost respect and sensitivity for her colleagues.

Unquestionably the major event of 1977 for Kiri was her first performance of the title role in Richard Strauss's opera *Arabella*, first at Covent Garden in July and then in a new production at the Houston Grand Opera in the United States in November. The year began in Paris, however, with another series of *Don Giovanni* performances, followed by a new production at the Opéra of Mozart's *The Magic Flute*, in which she sang Pamina in German for the first time. Rolf Liebermann, the Opéra's General Administrator, had originally hoped to persuade Ingmar Bergman, whose film version of *The Magic Flute* had been so successful, to produce it in Paris, but this had not proved possible and in the event the opera was staged by the Viennese team of Horst Zankl as director and Arik Brauer as designer, with the octagenarian Karl Böhm conducting. The eccentric staging, with its anatomical settings, proved a disaster with the Parisian audience and there was much booing at the first night curtain, though not for Kiri, who scored a personal triumph as Pamina.

Stanley Sadie was there for *The Times* and wrote in the paper the following week describing the various disasters that had beset that first night which included an unscheduled extra interval in Act 2 when the three Boys became stuck in their chariot suspended from the flies. He continued: 'That, however, came opportunely. The show had stopped anyway, for Kiri Te Kanawa had just sung "Ach, ich fühls" in a way that, very properly, drew from the audience a bout of frenzied, rhythmical applause. When she had first appeared on the stage in Act 1, fleeing from Monostatos, she had sung that soaring phrase in a way that sends thrills through the spine and turns grown men's knees (not only Mr Bernard Levin's) to jelly. "Ach, ich fühls" was characterized, to use inadequate descriptive critical terminology, by rich and intense tone, a precise placing of each note and phrase, and carefully timed and shaped cadences. It was a performance in thousands, because it remained simple while being exceptionally beautiful and deeply felt. And all this was matched, even surpassed, by her radiant singing of the glorious F major music at her union with Tamino – not to mention the equal radiance of her stage presence.'

The production had no fewer than eleven performances; during them Kiri went to Strasbourg to record *Così fan tutte* for Erato Records with the forces of L'Opéra du Rhin, under their director Alain Lombard. The cast had Frederica Von Stade as Dorabella and Teresa Stratas as Despina, with the young English tenor David Rendall singing Fernando, Philippe Hüttenlocher as Guglielmo and Jules Bastin as Don Alfonso. Although not a recording in the highest international class, it nevertheless has a refreshingly youthful atmosphere and Kiri sings Fiordiligi quite splendidly.

She returned to London in the last week of June to start rehearsals for *Arabella* at Covent Garden. She regards the role now as 'the hardest I've ever had to learn – it's so very difficult to remember. At the same time it's one of the most satisfying operas that I've done: I like the challenge. The character may not be as interesting as Elvira or Violetta, but musically it's very interesting indeed. Maybe it is a slightly boring opera at times and very long, but it's a connoisseur's piece.'

Arabella was the last opera Richard Strauss wrote in collaboration with his great librettist, Hugo von Hofmannsthal. In fact the librettist died suddenly of a stroke just after completing work, with the composer's telegram of thanks and congratulations lying unopened on the table in front of him. The opera was their joint attempt to provide a sequel to the enormously popular *Der Rosenkavalier*: it also was set in Vienna but a century later than that opera. Once again the subject was love and intrigue in Viennese society, but this time the faintly seedy tale of the bankrupt Count Waldner attempting to marry off his elder daughter to a rich husband in order to pay off his gaming debts, whilst bringing up the younger daughter disguised as a boy so as to save money, fails to engage one's interest and sympathy to the same degree as *Der Rosenkavalier*. Moreover, though there are passages of musical magnificence, particularly for Arabella herself, there are also extensive parts of the score which scarcely rise above the run-of-the-mill. Nevertheless it is a role which fits Kiri superbly. Firstly the music lies ideally for her voice, as does so much of Strauss's music; secondly the character of a straight-forward, unaffected, independent-minded young girl, who is at all times true to herself and yet retains a flirtatious sense of fun allied to a fundamental seriousness of purpose, could have been written with Kiri in mind.

The first performance was not achieved without difficulties. Kiri recalls, 'I was working with Richard Amner and ten days before the first night he said to me, "You're going to have to cancel – you can't remember it." I replied, "Don't ever say that to me – there's no such word as can't, and I'll prove I can do it." I called in Jean Mallandaine as well as Vera and we worked for five days non-stop: that was the new me – I'd never have managed it in my early days at the Opera Centre – and I learned it. I stayed put at Glyndebourne with Jean, and Vera even came and gave me lessons there. Now that it's in my head it'll probably stay there for good.'

The first night on 16 July went beautifully, sensitively con-ducted by Wolfgang Rennert, with Rudolf Hartmann's original production carefully and straightforwardly staged by Hans Hartleb. The strong cast included Ingvar Wixell as Madryka, Elizabeth Robson as Zdenka and Michael Langdon as Count Waldner. Kiri's appearance was not improved by a rather heavy blonde wig which sat too high on her forehead, but she moved with confidence, appeared thoroughly to understand the German she was singing, and sang quite beautifully. Once again the critics approved, William Mann writing in *The Times*: 'Within an already attractive background Kiri Te Kanawa poured out a rich, sensuous, steady soprano voice, new to the role, but greatly delectable. Her blonde wig does not become her, any more than the heavy make-up, but that does not prevent her from precipitating the action by her forthright character. The monologue "Mein Elemer" was gently and sensuously sung, likewise her part in the final staircase scene, as radiant and lovingly detailed as I can remember among all Arabellas in decades of devotion to the work.' Kiri couldn't complain about that, even though there were others, like Ronald Crichton in the *Financial Times*, who felt that her interpretation was as yet not fully developed.

In Houston four months later, with Jean Mallandaine, now the Houston Grand Opera's Music Adminstrator and Chief Coach, still there to help, Charles Mackerras couldn't believe that Kiri didn't actually speak German, so fluent was her mastery of the text. The production was by John Cox, with designs by Elisabeth Dalton, and Thomas Stewart sang Mandryka. Kiri felt more confident, so the performance went even better, though the orchestral playing in Houston was not as fine as it had been at Covent Garden.

This series of Arabella performances ended in the middle of November, and Kiri then returned to London to prepare her next new role – that of Rosalinde in Johann Strauss's *Die Fledermaus*. This multilingual New Year production was to be televised 'live' on its opening night, and beamed by satellite for reception in Europe and the United States as well, providing Kiri with the largest audience to which she had ever sung. Covent Garden had engaged Julia Trevelyan Oman as designer and Zubin Mehta to conduct, with the veteran Viennese director Leopold Lindtberg, who had been responsible for the Vienna State Opera's production of *Die Fledermaus* in 1960. Lindtberg was primarily a theatrical director and Kiri considered that he was insisting on far too much of the multilingual dialogue – hers in English, with occasional touches – on her own initiative – of an exasperated New Zealand accent; it tired her voice and held up the action. She also found him totally lacking in humour and very difficult to work with. Kiri says now that she told him, 'You've managed to make a reasonably happy cast thoroughly unhappy. He denied it, so I said, "Well, you haven't done a bad job then!" He made such heavy weather of the humour and didn't seem interested in the music at all. I couldn't stand the endless rehearsals and found the prospect of being broadcast and televised live quite terrifying.'

In the event the performances on New Year's Eve, though over-long with its guest appearances in the second act at Orlofsky's party by ballet dancers as well as Isaac Stern and Daniel Barenboim, went well; and Zubin Mehta's conducting injected a certain vigour into the proceedings. Despite her forebodings, Kiri turned in a most lovable characterization of Rosalinde and had an enormous success with the 'Czárdás' in Act 2, thoroughly approved in the press, as was her command of the dialogue. Nevertheless what should have proved an enjoyable experience for her was not, and she hasn't sung the role again: her only other appearance in Covent Garden's *Die Fledermaus* was as that 'surprise' guest at Orlofsky's party three years later.

12

A Film and A Wedding

FROM THE BEGINNING OF 1978 until now Kiri has consolidated her position as an international opera star, increasingly known and admired. In 1978 she sang Violetta in *La Traviata* at the Sydney Opera House conducted by Richard Bonynge in a new production by John Copley, based on the one he did for English National Opera in London, with beautiful designs by Michael Stennett. Working again with John Copley Kiri concentrated totally and responded completely to his direction with correspondingly impressive results. John Copley himself says, 'She's as tough as old boots if she needs to be, but her problem, I think, will always be her concentration. I'm deeply devoted to Kiri but she can still exasperate me more than anyone I work with! In *Figaro* at Covent Garden and in *La Traviata* in Sydney she couldn't have been more concentrated and brilliant, but there have been other times when I've worked with her and felt she wasn't totally there and that, good as she was, she could have been ten times better. But she'll always be a law unto herself – that's one of the most attractive things about her.' Full jumbo jets crossed the Tasman Sea bringing New Zealanders to hear her sing and to bemoan the fact that they still had no opera house in their own country in which to hear her, something that Kiri hopes eventually to help remedy. She sang Violetta, somewhat less successfully, at Covent Garden. Two difficulties occurred after a happy rehearsal period at the London Opera Centre: Kiri collapsed with a suspected chest infection during a rehearsal at Covent Garden two days after Christmas and only recovered in time for one final run-through of the opera, with piano, before the first performance on New Year's Day 1980; this, combined with an overtime ban by the Royal Opera House orchestra prevented any possibility of a dress rehearsal and led to a somewhat tentative opening night, though her interpretation strengthened noticeably as the opera's run continued.

She sang Amelia in *Simone Boccanegra* at La Scala, Milan at the end of 1978, four performances conducted by Claudio Abbado, with four different tenors and Piero Cappuccilli as Boccanegra. The audiences were a trifle cool, a reaction to some extent explained by the fact that Kiri had not fully understood the 'claque' system, and gave the claque leader only about £12 for the four performances, which caused Cappuccilli much amusement when she told him about it. Things went better when she sang the Countess in *Figaro* at the Salzburg Festival in 1979 with Herbert von Karajan conducting one of her four performances. The great maestro treated her with friendly courtesy but felt that in so short a period there was nothing he could, or should, do to alter her interpretation of the role of the Countess. Still, the experience left Kiri hoping that one day she would work with him again, preferably on a new production where he could rehearse her from scratch.

Two new productions at Covent Garden, *Simone Boccanegra* in the summer of 1980 and *Don Giovanni* a year later did not, despite favourable notices for her own performances, prove as successful as she had hoped. Nevertheless the *Boccanegra* performances, produced and designed somewhat wanly by Filippo Sanjust though most sensitively conducted by Colin Davis, and with the fine American baritone Sherrill Milnes in the title role, drew full houses. Sir John Tooley feels that 'if Kiri had not been in *Boccanegra* it very probably would not have sold out. When Kiri's name is on the boards, the public will buy the tickets: she has such tremendous pull with the public – they worship her.' One more reason for such loyalty stemmed from the fact that between one performance of *Boccanegra* on a Wednesday and the next on Saturday, Kiri at just a few hours' notice gave a memorably spontaneous and vivid performance of Mimì in Covent Garden's production of *La Bohème* on the Thursday when Mirella Freni was suddenly called home to Italy. John Tooley found it typical of her own loyalty to the house and to the audience. 'She agreed at once to do it and only had two requests: could we arrange a car to get her to and from the theatre as Des was due to be somewhere else, and could she have a particular prompter, in case she suddenly lost the words.' Despite the inevitable strain, Kiri gave a totally committed performance which fully merited the standing ovation she received at the final curtain.

After the performance, Kiri continued her love affair with the Paris Opéra, adding the Countess in *Figaro* to her three other Mozart roles there as well as singing the title role in Covent Garden's production of *Arabella* in the spring of 1981 when the projected Paris production of Gounod's *Romeo et Juliette*, in which she was to have sung Juliette, was abandoned at fairly short notice. Needless to say, Parisian critics and audiences alike revelled in the beauty, glamour and vocal mastery of the role of Arabella. It was also in Paris that she added her two newest roles to her repertory: the Marschallin in Strauss's *Der Rosenkavalier*, which she sang in December 1981 at the Théâtre des Champs Elysées while the Palais Garnier was closed for repairs, and Puccini's *Tosca*, back at L'Opéra, in March 1982. Her Marschallin was described as 'at the chrysalis stage' by Alan Blyth in the *Daily Telegraph*, and as 'a first draft' by John Higgins in *The Times*, but it already had the stamp of potential greatness. To add to her pleasure, her friend Frederica von Stade sang Octavian and Pierre Cardin threw a party for her at Maxim's during the opera's run.

In *Tosca*, a new production by Jean-Claude Auvray, conducted by Seiji Ozawa and with Ingvar Wixell as Scarpia, Kiri scored a personal triumph with the audience: there was a standing ovation for her at the first night's final curtain, and Basil Horsfield had never seen so many flowers in her dressing-room – 'like a Mafia funeral parlour'. John Higgins, writing the following week in *The Times*, though he thoroughly disliked Jean-Paul Chambas's sets, largely approved Auvray's production and had no doubts whatever about the success of Kiri's first Tosca. 'Kiri Te Kanawa, in a flowing yellow summer robe, makes a marvellous entrance. Her eyes dart around the church: piety demands that a statue of the madonna gets first attention with the bouquet of flowers, but then jealousy takes over rapidly as she sights Cavaradossi's painting. The second of her first-act exits was equally impressive: the chapel walls split open to reveal the nave of the church – a somewhat cardboardy structure – with a square of sunlight at the end, open-air protection against Scarpia's attentions. Miss Te Kanawa's voice was in lustrous tone, soaring easily with Puccini's vocal line which has always seemed to lie well for her. "Vissi d'arte" in the next act was sung not as a confession of Tosca's life style, but in a spirit of bitterness at the way fate has treated her: it was all there in the last couple of lines, with the final "Così" spat out in despair. After the delicate, soft opening, the aria went slightly askew on the first night, but the recovery was quick and Kiri Te Kanawa can already claim to be an outstanding Tosca.' He concluded his notice by observing: 'A stormy reception greeted the curtain on the first night, with the house apparently divided just about evenly between boos and counter cheers for the production team and for Seiji Ozawa, who took a long time to secure the right orchestra tension . . . But for the singers there was nothing but praise, especially for Kiri Te Kanawa. Jean-Claude Auvray has made some visual errors, but from his soprano he has secured an outstanding performance.' It was quite an accolade for her first attempt at one of opera's most demanding roles.

The New York Metropolitan saw her at the beginning of 1982 in a new production by Colin Graham and conducted by James Levine, of *Così fan tutte*, with Maria Ewing (who married Sir Peter Hall during the run) singing her sister Dorabella. The production was an enormous success, as was Kiri, and crowds would gather outside the Met's stage door in the Lincoln Center to see her leave.

Kiri has been busy outside the opera house as well. In the autumn of 1977 she toured Europe with Claudio Abbado and the Vienna Philharmonic Orchestra, singing Strauss's *Four Last Songs* and Mahler's 4th Symphony. For their last flight together Kiri bought seven or eight kilos of cake and served it to the orchestra, thus winning their undying devotion. A year later she set off with pianist Richard Amner for a series of song recitals with a programme of Schubert, Schumann, Richard Strauss, Hugo Wolf, Fauré, Duparc and William Walton, beginning in Poole and taking in Cardiff and the Royal Naval College Chapel at Greenwich on the way to Linz, Vienna and Paris – the Opéra – before ending at Covent Garden with a sold-out Royal Opera House. She recorded the programme for CBS; it was well received, as was her CBS recording of the *Four Last Songs* with the London Symphony Orchestra conducted by Andrew Davis, which won a 'Grammy' Award in the United States.

Of these two recordings the Strauss is the more completely successful and demonstrates Kiri's clear, creamy tone and pure, incisive delivery and phrasing at their very best. Although Alan Blyth, writing in *Gramophone* in May 1979 found her 'soaring tone and outgoing manner' were well matched to the songs of Strauss, he also found that in listening to Elisabeth Schwarzkopf's interpretations, 'I immediately recognized the difference between good singing and profound interpretation.' Nevertheless John Steane, that great expert on the recorded voice and author of *The Grand Tradition* which deals with seventy years of singing on record, felt otherwise. Though he too still regards Schwarzkopf as supreme, in a programme on BBC Radio 3 in which he studied Kiri's recorded output he remarked, 'Strauss might well have been dreaming of Te Kanawa when he wrote the *Four Last Songs*.' What is more, when he came to consider all available recorded versions of them on Radio 3's *Record Review* in April 1982, including Lisa Della Casa, Gundula Janowitz and Montserrat Caballé, he unhesitatingly placed Kiri as runner-up to Schwarzkopf's 1966 recording, conducted by Georg Szell. He agreed that her art had still fully to mature, but added, 'I hear people say about Kiri Te Kanawa, "Of course it's a lovely voice, but she doesn't know what she's singing about." I'd like them to test that not by hearsay, but by hear-sing. Her singing is beautifully and sensitively expressive and, to my mind, hers is the record which provides the strongest competition to Schwarzkopf and Szell.'

Kiri herself is the first to agree that there remains much to discover in these songs, and hopes she will have the opportunity to record them at least twice more in the course of her career, as her voice and understanding develop. As to her recital recording, although Steane, reviewing it in *Gramophone* in November 1979, found her singing 'lovely but lacking zest', this did not prevent Sir William Walton, in his appearance on *Desert Island Discs* on BBC Radio 4 to celebrate his 80th birthday in March 1982, from choosing her singing of his *Façade* song 'Old Sir Faulk' on this record to accompany him to his island, finding it the best performance he had heard in the sixty years since he had written it.

Kiri has not added to her recital repertory since the 1978 tour, and Vera does not really expect her to do so at present. Neither of them felt at first that she was temperamentally or intellectually fully attuned to this branch of the art of singing, but she has persevered and of late has found that it comes much more easily to her. She has, however, been busy in the recording studio. She added another recording of Elvira in *Don Giovanni* to the earlier one conducted by Colin Davis. This was for CBS, was conducted by Lorin Maazel and is the sound-track of Joseph Losey's film of the opera. She has also, finally in 1981, recorded her first major role, the Countess in *The Marriage of Figaro*, for Decca with Georg Solti conducting. Also during 1981, and also for Decca, she took part in an immensely enjoyable recording of *The Beggar's Opera*, singing as well as speaking quite splendidly the role of Polly Peachum, with Alfred Marks and Angela Lansbury as her parents, Joan Sutherland as Lucy Lockit and Richard Bonynge conducting. In more serious vein she has recorded the Beethoven Choral Symphony for EMI, with Eugen Jochum conducting the London Symphony Orchestra, the Brahms German Requiem in Chicago, with Solti conducting the Chicago Symphony – her solo here is quite ravishing – and Berlioz's song cycle *Les Nuits*

[171]

d'Été, with L'Orchestre de Paris conducted by Daniel Barenboim. For Decca she recorded one record of a five record set containing all Mozart's concert arias sung by Kiri and four other sopranos. This was conducted by Gyorgy Fischer.Most recently, for CBS, she has made an album of Verdi and Puccini arias, conducted by John Pritchard, and a complete recording of Puccini's rarely heard *La Rondine*, conducted by Lorin Maazel.

On the domestic front, too, life has flourished. To meet the needs of their expanding family the Parks moved early in 1978 to a larger house as their British base, more isolated and slightly deeper into Surrey. Tom Te Kanawa arrived from New Zealand, bearing his chain-saw, to mastermind the refurbishments and supervise the local team of builders, plumbers and electricians who tended to fall in love with Kiri at first sight and to go about their work whistling tunes from whatever opera she happens to be preparing at the time. Thomas Park, like his sister Toni, was baptised in the Catholic Actors' Church of Corpus Christi in Maiden Lane, Covent Garden by the Right Reverend Monsignor Frank Horsfield, Basil Horsfield's brother; needless to say Basil and John Davern stood as godfathers again. Another key change was Kiri and Desmond's acquisition of a house in the Algarve in Portugal – conveniently near to a golf course – so family holidays with the children could be spent in peace and quiet exactly when they wanted them.

Kiri has found herself the subject of ever-increasing interest from the press and media. In March 1980 she was the castaway on *Desert Island Discs* – she rather surprised Roy Plomley by choosing no operatic records at all, though she did select Mozart's Flute Concerto No. 1 so that 'I can do my Isadora Duncan to it'. On Christmas Eve 1980 she was seen on BBC television playing golf with Placido Domingo on the famous Wentworth Course. She had never played there, and took the engagement seriously enough to put in some concentrated practice with Desmond in advance. She won – of course – with Bernard Levin as her admiring caddy and Sir John Tooley performing that task for Placido. She is now scheduled to play a round with the top professional Peter Alliss for his television series too, though she is less confident of beating him. In March 1981 Kiri was a guest on Michael Parkinson's show on BBC television and finally, on Christmas Day 1981, she was the subject of *This Is Your Life* with Eamonn Andrews on Thames Television. Having been collared by Eamonn and most of the management of the Royal Opera House on the steps of St Paul's Cathedral, she was joined in the studio by Desmond, Tom Te Kanawa, and by her bridesmaid Sally Rush, and a very old friend, Kura Beale from North Island, who had known her since she was three, all of whom had been flown specially from New Zealand to join her on the programme. The Prince of Wales addressed a letter to the programme from Balmoral, 'to send my very best wishes to my favourite soprano on a special occasion and to say how much one of her greatest fans admires her glorious voice *and* her acting ability.' It ended with: 'PS. I hope this isn't too much of a shock for you!' Kiri was also joined on the programme by Harry Secombe, James Robertson, Colin Davis, Stuart Burrows, and Richard Baker, with filmed messages from Dame Sister Mary Leo, Dame Joan Sutherland from her dressing-room at San Francisco Opera and Sir Georg Solti. It was quite a line-up, quite a programme; Toni and Thomas made their first public appearances, which they carried off with aplomb. On the academic front too she has prospered, having thrice been awarded honorary doctorates of music, by Dundee, Durham and Oxford Universities, though she will be unable to attend Encaenia at Oxford and collect her degree until 1983. It's a fair achievement for a girl who left school in Auckland without a GCE 'O' Level to her name.

But two events above all have brought Kiri before a world-wide audience. The first was Joseph Losey's film of Mozart's *Don Giovanni*, made in Italy in the autumn of 1978, premiered in Paris, New York and Washington DC the following year, and finally arriving in Britain in the middle of 1980. The second, far wider-reaching event was signalled when in April 1981 she was chosen by the Prince of Wales to sing at his marriage to the Lady Diana Spencer in St Paul's Cathedral on Wednesday, 29 July 1981, an occasion that was watched by a televison audience of over 600 million people throughout the world.

Kiri's involvement in the film of *Don Giovanni* sprang from her work at the Paris Opéra and the admiration of its General Adminis-trator, Rolf Liebermann, for her performances there. Liebermann had set up the film project during 1977, and by the end of that year had both arranged the finance and persuaded Joseph Losey to direct. In fact this veteran of the cinema, famous for such films as *The Servant*, *The Go-Between* and *Secret Ceremony*, had never seen *Don Giovanni* staged in the opera house: his knowledge of the opera was confined to the pre-war recording made at Glyndebourne, con-ducted by Fritz Busch, which he often played and greatly liked. Thus it was Liebermann who, with Losey's agreement, took the early decisions to film the opera against a setting of Palladian villas in the Veneto, to use Lorin Maazel as the conductor (with CBS Records thus funding that side of the production) and to choose the cast – predominantly on voices, but secondly and importantly on looks. It was centred around Ruggero Raimondi as Don Giovanni; Leporello was José Van Dam, the American tenor Kenneth Riegel played Don Ottavio, John Macurdy the Commendatore and the young English singer, Malcolm King, was cast as Masetto. Amongst the ladies Kiri was, of course, Elvira; the German soprano Edda Moser was Donna Anna and Teresa Berganza, who had not sung the role before, was Zerlina.

The recording, as usual, came first; it took place in June 1978 at L'Eglise du Liban, the Lebanese church near the Panthéon, on the Left Bank and was produced by Paul Myers of CBS, though both Losey and Liebermann were constantly present during the often fraught recording sessions. Lorin Maazel was already heavily engaged in the new production of Verdi's *Luisa Miller* at Covent Garden, and was commuting between Paris and London, eternally short of time. His reading of the music reflects this, having a relent-less, hard-driven quality which leaves one speculating on what Colin Davis or John Pritchard might have done with the project. As tempers grew frayed, and dismay increased at the cavernous acoustic

[174]

of the church, which was in due course transmitted to the film's sixteen-track Dolby sound, Kiri recalls that it was Kenneth Riegel who kept them all amused with such cracks as, 'Glitter and be gay — remember this is Hollywood, darling!'

Once recording was completed there was a break before the cast moved on to Vicenza at the end of September for filming. The orchestra and conductor, of course, did not go to Italy; only harpsichordist Janine Reiss accompanied them to play the recitatives 'live', trundling from one location to another on the back of a jeep. The rest of the opera — arias and ensembles — was mimed by the singers to a play-back of their recording. Time was short as the budget for so specialized an undertaking was relatively low, at four million dollars. Despite this the six weeks allocated for filming had to be stretched to eight, and the budget crept over the six million dollar mark. Part of the reason for this was the weather, unreasonably cold and wet for early autumn in the Veneto. Kiri recalls, 'They used fake rain for one scene, and then we were actually rained off for five days! It was also absolutely frigid there, particularly in the makeup-room — it was in one of the beautiful Palladian villas, its walls covered with frescoes, and gas canister heaters had to be brought in to prevent us from freezing to death!'

Before the arrival of the cast in September, Losey had assembled a group of local Italian actors to perform his interpretation of the drama to a background of the recording. He had also sent to each singer his notes of advice on their characters: because of their other commitments there would be no time for another get-together between the end of recording and the first day of filming, and once filming had begun the budget allowed for no rehearsal time what-ever. Once shooting did begin Kiri remembers it as, 'The hardest work I ever did. We'd start early in the morning and finish late at night. The sun rose and set at its appointed times, but we never noticed. There was nothing called breakfast, lunch, or dinner: a meal was simply provided a certain number of hours after we'd been on the set.'

In fact, Losey interrupted very little during the shooting. 'If

[175]

Joe could see you were getting upset, he'd walk off with you for a chat, and everyone else just had to sit around and drink coffee until he brought you back.' Kiri responded very powerfully to Losey's direction; he in turn found that Kiri had marvellous dramatic instincts. 'Her big problem,' he told me later in Paris, 'was that if the camera wasn't actually on her, and she wasn't in the forefront of the action, she'd tend to lose concentration and look lost.' This was something that Peter Hall had observed many years before: 'Everybody has a centre, and I think Kiri's centre is her feet. If she's not fully involved, a weariness comes over her as she moves. But once she gets the feeling of a part, then the energy springs from her feet. In the film of *Don Giovanni* there's a bit when she's stumbling along, and I know she didn't know at that moment what she was doing.'

For opera singers, used to long rehearsals, the takes seemed very short, but then they came to dread the re-takes. 'There were twenty-two re-takes for one scene,' Kiri says now. 'After that, if it got beyond five, we'd all become manic, feeling, "If I let that person down it'll be Take 6, and then on into double figures." We'd all watch each other; nobody could bear to do more than three takes. The filming of my aria "Mi tradì" took from 6 a.m. until 7 p.m., and that was fast – they'd expected it to take two days. In fact all the discomfort and anxiety seemed to work: I think the best scene I did was the balcony scene at the beginning of the second act and it worked because I was in a raging temper, freezing cold, very worried, terribly nervous and utterly miserable!'

Kiri is almost certainly the film's greatest, most widely acclaimed success. She looks quite breathtakingly beautiful, wearing her costumes superbly, she sings magnificently and imbues Elvira with all the volatile, obsessive, passionate sexuality that she has always believed the character possesses. It is a portrayal far removed from the conventional image of opera where singers simply stand and deliver: her Elvira is a real, hot-blooded human being, a woman with whose passions an audience can and does identify, an image that is slow to fade. The first time I saw the film, in Paris, I asked the young French girl sitting beside me in the interval if she had ever been to the opera before. 'Yes,' she replied, 'but if only the opera was like this – this is so exciting!'

Joseph Losey's *Don Giovanni* displeased nearly all the music critics, who found it wilful, wayward, over-decorated and eccentric. But it appealed to the film critics, who found it excellent cinema; and above all it appealed to audiences, who at one time were queuing to see it in six different Paris cinemas, thus fulfilling Losey's aim to reach the huge audience of people who have never seen, or even heard, an opera. As he said to me the day after I had seen the film in Paris: 'I reckon my film has already been seen by more people in the cinema than in all the opera houses of the world since Mozart first staged *Don Giovanni* in 1787.'

On a sunny afternoon at the beginning of August 1981 Kiri sat in the garden of her house in Surrey, with her daughter Toni, now blonde, beautiful, and nearly five, beside her. She looked up at her mother and said, 'You look so tired – but don't worry, we're going on holiday this week – at last.' Toni was right: Kiri looked absolutely exhausted, and had every reason to do so. Up to the middle of June it had been a normal busy year, with a revival of *Così fan tutte* at Covent Garden in January, some television work in February and the recording of *The Beggar's Opera* in London during March. Towards the end of that month she had travelled to Paris to prepare a series of ten performances of *Arabella* during April and early May at the Opéra, during which period she also recorded Berlioz's *Les Nuits d'Été* with Daniel Barenboim. On her return to England she had recorded *The Marriage of Figaro* with Georg Solti for Decca, with Thomas Allen as the Count, Samuel Ramey as Figaro, Lucia Popp as Susanna, and her old friend Flicka von Stade singing Cherubino, as at Santa Fe a decade earlier when they were both new on the scene.

Then, at the end of June, Kiri had gone into rehearsal for Covent Garden's new production of *Don Giovanni*, the centre-piece of the Royal Opera's Mozart Festival, and the pace of life changed entirely. She was to give seven performances of *Don Giovanni*, plus four of *Così fan tutte*, between 6 and 25 July, with the marriage of Prince

Charles and the Lady Diana Spencer in St Paul's Cathedral just four days later. Talking of the Mozart Festival now that it was all over, she commented, 'It was the most stupid and ridiculous thing I've ever done in my entire life, and I'll never ever do it again. But I wanted to do it – I had to because I want Covent Garden always to be my home house. Stuart Burrows, Tom Allen, Richard Van Allan and I called ourselves the suicide quartet, the Kamikaze Squad, who were appearing in more than one opera at the same time. But I think that in singing Elvira and Fiordiligi on alternate nights, I had the hardest job of all.'

For the first time ever when singing at Covent Garden Kiri had moved out of home and into the Savoy Hotel, for the duration of the run. Usually she drives herself up and down from Surrey in one of the two small, rather battered cars that are the Park family's unpretentious form of transport, but this time she felt that the strain of travelling each day on top of her work at the Opera House would be too much for her. 'I'd decided the year before that I'd move into the Savoy for the Festival – I needed to be quiet and away from the telephone, otherwise I wasn't going to make it. Hardly anyone knew I was there, and the hotel had orders to tell anyone who did phone that I wasn't staying there. Des came to nearly every performance, which was very nice, and we would go back to the hotel and have little suppers after the performance. Then he'd go back home to the children, and I'd lock myself up in my tiny room until it was time to go back on stage again.'

In addition to pressure of work, there was pressure of another kind. The media naturally took enormous interest in her forthcoming appearance at St Paul's Cathedral, and the Royal Opera's press office was besieged by journalists demanding interviews. Katharine Wilkinson, the press officer, sorted that one out very neatly. The Thursday afternoon before the wedding, when Kiri still had two Mozart operas to go before the end of the Festival, a special press conference for Kiri was held in the crush bar. It was well attended, not merely by British newspapers and television, but by Tom Brokaw of Americas' NBC *Today* programme, Judith Fife of

Radio New Zealand, a representative of Australian Television's Channel 10, and many European journalists as well. Although Kiri felt 'yet another ounce of my energy was being drained out of me', she looked remarkably poised and assured, carrying her 'wedding dress' specially created for her by Léonard in a bag, having been earlier that afternoon to Philip Somerville, the milliner, choosing a hat to set it off. She fielded all questions, both sensible and foolish, with courtesy and charm and, as usual, won the hearts of the assembled audience.

Kiri regards the invitation to sing at the royal wedding now as the chance of a lifetime. 'Prince Charles could have chosen anybody in the world to sing at his wedding. I never realized we'd both be invited as guests at the wedding as well or that Des and I would be invited to the ball at Buckingham Palace on Monday night, which was truly wonderful. I'd started rehearsing straight after the final performance of *Don Giovanni* on the Saturday night and, of course, had two singing lessons with Vera! I hadn't sung "Let the bright seraphim" for a long time, but it is a lovely aria, Prince Charles had chosen it and I had to do it well. I stayed at the Savoy again the night before, arrived at St Paul's in plenty of time, and took along my little flask of iced water and my sweeties, so my throat wouldn't dry up. An equerry had reminded me to have only one cup of tea for breakfast as there weren't any loos in St Paul's! I thought the aria went all right, and afterwards I had to get quickly to the television studio that had been set up near Buckingham Palace. I couldn't find my own car and driver in the crush, but fortunately two City of London policemen in a panda car recognized me and offered me a high-speed lift. In return I gave them my Order of Service which I signed for them; I discovered that it was sold the following month for £500 at a police auction, to raise money for the Mitcham Amateur Boxing Association. We went to lunch after that and then again to the BBC studios for *Nationwide*. As we walked through Green Park on our way to lunch everybody seemed to recognize me, and wanted to photograph me with their children. Later, in the evening, Des and I went over to Basil and John's house to talk about everything, and stayed till midnight. It was a wonderfully happy day – one of the happiest days of my life.'

The Prince of Wales first heard Kiri sing at the royal concert in Dunedin, New Zealand in March 1970, but he admits now, 'At that time she was comparatively unknown to me – though not to New Zealand of course. For me she was just a soprano who sang beautifully at the concert: I hadn't become particularly interested in opera at that stage.' In England he first saw her at Glyndebourne, singing the Countess in *Figaro* in 1974, and next in *Così fan tutte* at Covent Garden in 1976. Since then he has tried to attend as many of her performances at Covent Garden as possible. He finds that, 'What is so marvellous about her is that not only is her voice growing to such stature, but so are her looks – she becomes more and more attractive as she goes on. Each time I saw her I realized that here was somebody who was superb: not only from the singing point of view but from her presence on stage which, to my way of thinking, is one of the most essential qualities in order for an audience to appreciate opera. The thing which riveted me about Kiri was her effortless quality. You can sit back and enjoy it, feeling she is totally in command of the whole situation.'

The Prince went to see *Don Giovanni* at Covent Garden just a few days before his wedding and thought, 'It was the best of all, the most exciting and enjoyable opera I've been to so far – and I've been to quite a few now. I enjoyed it so much mainly because the acting was so outstanding, you actually felt yourself involved in the plot. I loved the way Kiri did Elvira – she was so wonderfully sexy and seductive which gave it so much more of a believable quality.'

With such enthusiasm for her work, it was hardly surprising that the Prince of Wales chose Kiri to sing at his wedding. 'I always wanted somebody to sing at my wedding, always wanted it to be a marvellous musical occasion. It was just a question of who was going to be the right person to sing. Having talked over the whole musical aspect with Sir David Willcocks of the Bach Choir and Sir John Tooley of the Royal Opera House, the general feeling was,

"Let's ask Kiri" – she was, in everybody's opinion, the best; and of course the other thing I terribly wanted was that it should be somebody from Britain or the Commonwealth; that was very important to me. She might have been anywhere in the world at the time, but she was in London and, to my amazement, she accepted.'

The choice of music was also something which the Prince discussed with Willcocks and Tooley. '"Let the bright seraphim" was one of the pieces they suggested as a possibility. There were one or two things that I suggested which they didn't think were suitable! When you're trying to choose something for a cathedral and a wedding and a religious service, it's quite difficult to find something that fits. You couldn't really have something from an opera because it wouldn't be quite right; so of course it boiled down to Handel, because he's absolutely marvellous.'

Since Kiri sang while the Prince and Princess of Wales were signing the register after the service, Prince Charles could only just hear her. 'It was a marvellous sound, coming through naturally; and I found it almost more exciting to hear it, slightly disembodied, from the other side of the Cathedral, where we were. But, remember, we were signing the Register at the time, and after a wedding everybody tends to be hugging and kissing each other!' In fact Kiri was singing in the North Transept of St Paul's while the register was being signed in the Dean's Aisle, fully fifty yards away across the Cathedral. The Prince loved her dress and hat. 'It was marvellous – like a wonderful canary or budgerigar – a stunning combination of colours. I think she looks wonderful anyway, and looking at the tape of our wedding again the other night, what appealed to me so much is that she always looks so happy, and radiates this great enjoyment. Even at the wedding, where she must have been fairly nervous, she looked splendid and smiled hugely, which communicated itself to everyone.'

Kiri's true secret has always been, right from the outset, that ability to communicate her sheer enjoyment of singing to everybody, wherever and whenever she has sung.

ACKNOWLEDGEMENTS

This book was to have been written by Sidney Edwards, but first his heavy schedule as Arts Editor of the *Evening Standard* and then his tragically early death in 1979 prevented his getting beyond the planning stage. His two draft chapters were nevertheless of much assistance to me over Kiri's early life and career, as was Norman Harris's short, illustrated book *Kiri – Music and a Maori Girl*, published in New Zealand by A. H. & A. W. Reed in 1966. It was Kiri's managers, Basil Horsfield and John Davern, who first suggested that I should take on the book, and I am greatly indebted to them, both for their faith in me and for their enormous help and encouragement once I started work. Without the resources of their knowledge and of their office, under the efficient control of Rene Brown and Gaby Israel, this book could never have been written.

It could not even have been started without the full co-operation of Kiri herself, and of Desmond. I received from both of them throughout encouragement, help, friendship and hospitality. Desmond and his hyper-efficient filing-system frequently came to my rescue, invariably managing to find just the press cutting, programme or photograph I needed. He worked so hard that there were times when I felt that he was doing everything for this book except actually writing it. Kiri too, despite an invariably packed schedule, gave up much time and energy to the project. Her patience during our early interviews was well-nigh inexhaustible and thereafter, whenever she was back in England, she found time to bring me up-to-date. Both she and Desmond painstakingly read my various drafts, offered useful criticism and carefully corrected any errors of detail. Such mistakes as remain are thus entirely mine.

I am deeply grateful to all those busy people who found time to give me interviews. It is perhaps a measure of Kiri's popularity that professional people, however busy, were so keen to help. The following were of particular assistance to me and I remain in their debt: Tom Te Kanawa,

Raewyn Blade, Betty Hanson, Robert Hanson, June Hall, James Robertson, Veronica Haigh, Jean Mallandaine, Vera Rozsa, John Copley, Frederica von Stade, John Blatchley, Elaine Steabler, Norman Feasey, Albert Wheeler, Jason Soifer, Tom Hawkes, Sir John Tooley, Sir Colin Davis, Sir Peter Hall, Anne Howells, Stuart Burrows, John Pritchard, David Harper, Joseph Losey, James Tuplin, Sally Rush and Kura Beale. These last two ladies arrived in London through the good work of Maurice Leonard, researcher and writer of Thames Television's *This Is Your Life* programme about Kiri; his research was of enormous advantage to me at a crucial stage and he gave of it unstintingly. From New Zealand Dame Sister Mary Leo and Barbara Brown wrote me long and informative letters about their dealings with Kiri in her early career. Finally, and vitally for the last chapter, His Royal Highness The Prince of Wales most kindly consented to give me an immensely useful interview.

Many of my colleagues in musical journalism put their extensive knowledge of Kiri's career at my disposal and I am particularly grateful to Harold Rosenthal, Alan Blyth, Noel Goodwin, John Higgins, Desmond Shawe-Taylor, William Mann, Stanley Sadie and Elizabeth Forbes. At Covent Garden the Royal Opera's indefatigable, and ever enthusiastic press officer, Katharine Wilkinson, and her assistant Jane, were invariably at hand to help me out of difficulties, arrange interviews, provide photographs and give much appreciated encouragement.

Needless to say I am also deeply grateful to Robin Baird-Smith and Gill Gibbins at Collins, and to my endlessly sympathetic and constructive agent, Andrew Hewson. There were times when my other professional activities and commitments made me feel that this book would never be finished. The patience and support of all three ensured that it was. I also owe much gratitude to Amanda Beresford who painstakingly, speedily and accurately typed transcripts of my taped interviews. In addition a number of my friends were good enough to read sections of my typescript and to offer useful comments, and there were other friends who assisted in other, equally valuable ways. Amongst them I am especially indebted to James Morton, David Barr, David Blow, Barry Jackson, Pam Long, Carla Heffner, Claudio Stern and Penny Lloyd. Pat, Ursula and Heather Murphy also gave me encouragement, not least by lending me their flat in Roquebrune-sur-Argens, where I spent five weeks preparing the early stages of the book and where I was offered kind support by Humphrey and Christina Burton, whose house was in a nearby village and who prevented me from despairing.

Finally, nothing could have been achieved without the constant support, encouragement and constructive criticism of my wife, Clare Colvin. Her professionalism and skill have always been invaluable to me, and I am forever grateful to her for these, as for everything else. I only hope she feels this book will be worth its sometimes difficult gestation.

LONDON, MAY 1982

INDEX

David Fingleton first became interested in music through going to Ernest Read Children's Concerts while at his prep school, and went on to discover a passion for opera. After reading modern history at Oxford he began to practice at the Criminal Bar and took up musical journalism as a working hobby. In 1970 he created an opera column for *Tatler and Bystander* which he continued to write until 1979. He was an Associate Editor of *Music and Musicians* and has written for the *Guardian* and the *Evening News,* where his Music Man column appeared every Friday during the last year of the paper's life. He has occasionally given radio talks on musical topics and is State Design Correspondent of *Arts Review.* He left the Bar to become a Metropolitan Stipendiary Magistrate in 1980, and is currently the music critic for the *Daily Express.* He has admired Kiri Te Kanawa's work since first hearing her sing in 1969 and has known her for nearly ten years. He is married to the arts journalist Clare Colvin.